Dear Reader

I'm proud to say this book is being republished in my name: Lindsey Elms on 6|10|24.

As I had some copies of this 1st edition left, it felt right to pay them forward - please do the same ♡

I hope you find some insights within its pages.

May you always be guided by love

Lindsey
- x -

lindseyelms. com

GUIDED BY

Love

A FIRST AID KIT FOR YOUR BROKEN HEART

AVA WOODS

BALBOA.PRESS

A DIVISION OF HAY HOUSE

Balboa Press books may be ordered through booksellers or by contacting:

Balboa Press
A Division of Hay House
1663 Liberty Drive
Bloomington, IN 47403
www.balboapress.co.uk
UK TFN: 0800 0148647 (Toll Free inside the UK)
UK Local: (02) 0369 56325 (+44 20 3695 6325 from outside the UK)

Print information available on the last page.

ISBN: 978-1-9822-8760-3 (sc)
ISBN: 978-1-9822-8761-0 (e)

Balboa Press rev. date: 10/14/2023

"My capability to tune into the energy of love gives me the words I need when I am ready to speak up, the compassion I need to forgive, and the power I need when I am lost."

-Gabrielle Bernstein, The Universe Has Your Back

CONTENTS

Part 5 – Paths to clarity

FOREWORD

I am Mandy Nicholson, and I am a Creative Genius Consultant, Artist, Author, and Creative Retreat owner who helps creative women launch, grow and scale their businesses, and make more money.

I was lucky enough to meet Ava via the online space when she booked a Discovery Call with me and subsequently joined my Creative Mastermind program. Through working together on her business and spending time together during a retreat at my creative space in Scotland, we have built a special relationship.

Ava is a truly loving and kind soul who has a passion for helping others, so when she discussed writing this book, I was her biggest cheerleader.

I have seen the power of the help Ava offers to others through her holistic 9 Star Ki approach, coupled with her own intuitive and empathic skills. The personal journey of learning she has experienced through life's challenges has enhanced her ability to connect with and coach others. Her gentle and loving nature makes her a real joy to work with and this book is packed to the brim with her personal magic and genuine love for her fellow humans.

The pain of losing her marriage has enhanced her ability to help others face and deal with their pain. Learning to not only cope, but to thrive during such a difficult time has fine-tuned her skills and allowed her to create a wonderful first aid kit for those in pain from a broken heart.

Ava has written this book so beautifully; you can almost feel the love oozing from the pages. Her own journey is honestly portrayed and used incredibly well to demonstrate how others can navigate their pain. Her writing skills will take you on the journey with her. You will laugh, cry, smile and feel the hope and opportunity in every carefully crafted word.

What impresses me most, and I am sure will impress you, is Ava's thirst for knowledge and answers. They say knowledge is power and the consistent effort she had demonstrated around her subject is equivalent to a PhD in life (my opinion not a scientific fact). You are in good and gentle hands when you are in Ava's world, absorb the lessons like she has and allow yourself to be healed.

My involvement in this book has been the best kind, I was asked to read it. I have watched Ava's journey, been there when she needed me and now had the privilege of being invited to read the book and write this foreword. My final comment to you, the reader is this...enjoy the gifts this book will bring into your life and immerse yourself in its pages. You won't regret it.

Mandy Nicholson BA, BSc

PREFACE

I sat in my car as the wind howled around me. I could hear trees falling and the rain battering my windscreen. It was pitch black and bitterly cold. Inside my car I was shivering; not only from the cold but also from the shock. My body reeling from the news, my heart breaking. I sat trying to shake it off like a bad dream. I thumped the steering wheel angrily, wailing, sobbing and despairing.

What was I going to do? How could this be happening?

It was the worst storm we had had in a decade; it was also the evening of my 20th Wedding Anniversary the night my husband, out of the blue, told me he was leaving.

Waves of shock and panic rippled through me. My stomach felt like the inside of a washing machine spin cycle. The intensity of my feelings gained momentum as my heart pounded faster and faster almost beating out of my chest.

The weather outside so obviously reflecting my internal emotions. The destruction of the storm echoing the destruction of my life.

The man who I thought was my soul mate, who I would grow old and wrinkly with had decided to leave me, our kids, our home and move to the other end of the country. It may have been the other end of the world.

Of course, like every marriage we had our share of challenges, none though that I thought were insurmountable. Sometimes I forgot to do the washing up, sometimes he forgot to get a card. We had grown up together and our partnership had made us better people. Every day there was a check in call from him and I'd get a schoolgirl sense of excitement when his car pulled onto the drive.

This was the man I was so connected to that we simultaneously chose the same Christmas lights at different shops on the same evening.

And yet there he was shoving a few items of clothes into a bag, whilst I followed him around the house like a lost sheep trying to get him to talk to me, to make sense of what was going on. Him looking up at me with a teary blank face saying, *"I've made my choice; I just have to go."*

I felt my entire world crumble apart.

I had wanted so badly to prove to our kids, Alfie and Iris, that love can endure, to spare them the heartache of parents separating. I felt I had failed them and my future grandchildren.

For the last few years, I had tried to fix the subtle grumblings of his discontent, whilst at the same time coming to recognise mine. I felt that love conquers all, believed that marriage is worth fighting for. Both of us had experienced the loss and disempowerment of our parents divorcing, I hung on with all my might for our children not to have the same fate.

The pain and grief of this earthquake ripping through my life was unbearable. After watching him leave, I realised life was presenting me with a choice- to stay bound and stuck in anger and disappointment or I could pick myself up, dust myself off and choose love.

Up to this point, my beliefs and expectations were like fairy tales, romantic notions. I thought that my marriage would be lifelong, that all obstacles could be overcome and that we would find a way to be besotted with each other again. Choosing love meant unbinding myself from old expectations of who I was and how I show up in the world.

I learnt a new way of viewing love that involved healthier boundaries, self-empowerment, and compassion for myself. Choosing love was an invitation to live a truly Soul-led life, grounded in self-belief. Amidst the pain and grief of separation it was my lighthouse. A beacon of light, rising out of the darkness. A tall and stable safe harbour for my tumultuous sea of emotions.

Walking down this new unexplored, path guided by love was a process. Although I did not know where the path would take me, it felt right. I felt completely supported and safe. Every turn has offered me a friendly ear, a warm hug of encouragement and lucky synchronicities that have propelled me forward, have held my resolve, my focus and encouraged me not to dwell.

Each step invited layers of me to be released. It was like I'd been wrapped up for years under many layers and as I walked, I discarded one item at a time leaving a trail behind me. Each item discarded left me feeling lighter, freer, and more peaceful. Ultimately, I became comfortable in my own skin, accepting of my true nature freckles and all. I know in my bones that I am lovable and that I have a beautiful love to give and share. I also knew I had to shed the layers that did not serve me.

The layers had kept me warm and cosy all these years, or so I'd thought. In fact, the warm fluffy scarf of not speaking up for my needs and wants had been strangling me. The heavy, waterproof coat had protected me from accessing my true feelings instead of allowing my tears to flow easily. The belt around my waist was a tourniquet for keeping 'everything together' even though it pinched.

Now I walk with a spring in my step, with my head held high. I feel light and free like a summer dress, blowing in the gentle breeze, unencumbered by expectations, and allowing my creativity full freedom of expression.

When the waves of emotion rise, I simply notice them, observe them, and let them take their natural course. Sometimes they crash to the shore, other times they gently ripple, caressing the sand. I am nurturing, compassionate and kind towards myself. I feel a wonderful sense of calm, with a constant subtle hum of loving support that is inside and outside of me all at once.

Life occasionally offers you the chance to contract, pause and expand once again. To bring you back into alignment with the truth of who you are. To love yourself and your life more than you dreamed possible, often when you least expect it.

Adapting to change can be a daunting prospect and yet I believe you are always supported and guided. That you are never given more than you can handle. And that if you allow yourself to be open and curious, life will show you the way.

You have within yourself all that you need to thrive. All the answers are within, truly they are. You are uniquely qualified to shine brightly as there is no other you. Being born with natural talents and the keys to unlock them is something you may not have been aware of until now. It's often the way; when you are naturally good at something, you may not be fully aware of it until someone, or something enlightens you or forces your hand.

The good news is that clues are everywhere and can be found in plain sight if you know what to look for. Sometimes they even literally fall into your lap.

INTRODUCTION

Where my writing journey began

For as long as I can remember I have always wanted to understand myself and others, to appreciate how we 'tick'. I have an innate curiosity and drive to connect on a deep level with myself and others. To be the best version of me that I can be.

In 2012 I attended a conference in Glasgow called "I Can Do It" organised by the book publishing company Hay House. I listened to and then met some amazing inspirational teachers including Louise Hay, Wayne Dyer, Cheryl Richardson, and Neil Donald Walsh.

Whilst looking around the vast bookshelves in the conference bookshop laden with wise words, a book literally fell off the stand in front of me and landed at my feet. It was like this book was so eager for me to read it, it had to make itself known. I was so pleasantly surprised by its invitation that I picked it up and bought it. Whilst still smiling over this encounter another book caught my attention and it is these two books in particular that have inspired my journey since then.

The books are, Blue Marsden's Soul Contract and Jean Hanner's Your Hidden Symmetry. I'd encourage you to read them.

I'd like to invite you on a journey of self-discovery. A journey from disconnection to connection, betrayal to self-love, guided by love and underpinned by nature's infinite wisdom.

This book is a gift of love from me to you. Within it you will discover some ways you disconnect from your true self and how to reconnect with yourself and others. I offer you some tools and exercises on how to keep in alignment with your own personal integrity, how to focus on and move forward with your life and feel a true sense of peace.

I will describe the 9 Key Self-Soothing tools to motivate positive thoughts and behaviours. You will discover your Nine Star Ki archetype and all its associated gifts. I will also explain how to work with the energy of your 9 Year Cycle to empower and enhance your life.

HOW TO USE THIS BOOK

There are moments in this book where I will invite you to participate.

Adults gain much more from practising the skills they have learnt and utilising ideas, than from reading alone. It would make my heart sing to know that this book has a positive influence on your life, that it has practical usefulness as well as offers support, comfort, and insights.

You can read the book from cover to cover, reading each chapter in turn; soaking up the stories, lessons, and healing.

You can intuitively flip to a page by asking a question, closing your eyes, flicking through the pages, and stopping when it feels right. Then study the guidance on the page you have chosen.

There are 3 directions in the book:

Take 5 Pause and Practice

Take 5 Pause and Act

Take 5 Pause and Journal

Take 5 Pause and Practice encourages you to practice a tool or exercise I have offered to enhance your experience, learning and growth.

Take 5 Pause and Act invites you to take an action such as playing a game.

Take 5 Pause and Journal invites you to take out a journal or notepad and give yourself some space and time to write down your unedited thoughts and feelings.

There are stories in the book where I share my experiences, some of which may be emotive for you. I felt it was important to dig deep into my emotions and share my truth intimately and candidly. I wrote this book for you as you may not have the words to describe your experience and yet they may be echoed through mine, bringing you insights, clarity and faith for a bright future.

I consider the journey I've been on a gift; I was set free because my Soul knew that I was abandoning myself in my marriage. I treasure the lessons I have learnt because I was able to create my life anew. A life where I can hear my truth and follow my heart's desires with confidence.

This is possible for you too.

Love and hugs

Ava x

Part 1
CYCLES OF CHANGE

1

CYCLES

You are influenced by and connected to many different cycles in life. From planetary and astronomical events- e.g., the moon which affects the tides, climate and weather- to biological- e.g., the menstruation cycle. Knowing that nothing lasts forever and is part of an ever-evolving cycle of change offers a light at the end of the tunnel. Even if life is tough right now, this too shall pass.

Following a seismic shift in your life, you can feel uncertain about who you are, what you have to offer, and what the future holds. Within this book I share how you can make good use of the cycles in your life. You'll learn how to move with the energy, not against it and to feel the power and freedom of recognising where you are placed.

You are a part of nature and are deeply intertwined and connected to her. Once you recognise her hidden codes and are familiar with how they are imprinted within you, she can open a whole new world to you. Nature has rhythms and predictable patterns which when viewed through certain lenses, give you a deep understanding of yourself. A view that enables you to shine brightly, design your life effectively and be in alignment with your true self.

I personally have been supported and guided by an ancient map based on cosmic cycles that has enabled me to make sense of who I am, where I am and where my strengths lie. I'm delighted that you now have access to this wisdom too. It's called Nine Star Ki and we'll delve into it shortly.

You have a choice

When my twenty-year marriage ended abruptly, I made a choice to focus on love. To make choices and decisions from the heart, from love not fear. There were so many paths I could have gone down- anger, rage, bitterness and yet I knew that only love would set me free. My training in Reiki, mindfulness and Nine Star Ki has taught me that your power is in the present moment. Change happens in the here and now. You have the power to choose who you are and what you stand for. To be so rooted in your truth that you will not allow it to be overridden by other people or circumstances.

That single choice enabled me to move through the devastation, grief and change without getting stuck. Instead, I experienced pauses and periods of time where I immersed myself in the feelings and thoughts that came up and allowed them to flow through me. To adapt, heal and grow.

I believe that cycles are a gift, opportunities to begin again in new empowered ways with the benefit of insight and growth. Some things are inevitable such as birth, death, the sun rising in the morning and the changing of the seasons. Life and the predictable natural passages of time do not wait; they march on whether we're ready or not, whether we want them to or not.

Choices are born from the awareness of new possibilities and perceptions. They can be intuitive, intellectual or learnt. They can be instantaneous or creep up on you over time. As the saying goes, it's easy when you know how. In the following chapters I will guide you through some insightful ways to make choices in life and relationships. To empower you and to support you.

Let's start with Nine Star Ki.

Nine Star Ki

I discovered many years ago, a map for life called Nine Star Ki. It shepherds you through the ever-changing energies and intricacies of life. It offers a blueprint for predictable patterns that show you how you are influenced by nature's cycles and how you can utilise this knowledge to gain greater levels of self-awareness and love.

Nine Star Ki (*ki* meaning energy) is the oldest form of knowledge about how energy moves through time. It is thought to be over 12,000 years old. Ancient peoples were very observant of their environment and intuitively understood that the astronomical cycles, seasons and climate influenced life on Earth, and planned their lives accordingly. From when and where they planted crops to which direction to build their homes in. They also noted that the timing of your birth has a great influence on your character.

You are made of energy

Everything in the Universe is made of energy including you. Energy has many names including *ki, chi*, Life-force, Spirit, Light, Aura and vibration or vibe. The name you know it by is not important- what matters is that you recognise it.

It's energy that gives you a zest for life, a sparkle in your eyes and the motivation to deal with tough things. When someone comes up behind you and you 'sense' them before they move or speak, you are sensing their energy.

You can feel the energy in a room when there has been an argument- the phrase 'you could cut the tension with a knife' comes to mind as the energy of anger is palpable. Equally the feeling of an awesome party where everyone is having fun can immediately lift your spirits and encourage you to join in.

Yin and Yang

One of the main foundational principles of Nine Star Ki is the concept of Yin and Yang, the feminine and masculine forces of nature. These energies represent the opposites in nature which are needed for creation, movement and balance. The two energies of Yin and

3

Yang meet in an everlasting dance, towards balance so there is never stillness, always movement. In practical terms, opposites offer insights and help us to discern. For example, knowing love is only possible when you experience the absence of it, feeling judged shows you how to be kind, feeling stressed can alert you to returning to calm and peace.

Day always fades into night. There are active times and times to simply be and receive. There are moments when things contract and expand again like relationships, the rhythm of your heart and breathing.

Often when you feel like taking a certain action, the more effective approach is to do the opposite. For example, when you are feeling angry with someone and want to shout and scream at them. The more productive approach is to sit with the anger, to let it flow and take its course. Then respond instead of reacting. That way you have a much better chance of your needs and emotions being understood and met.

For example, instead of running away or hiding from an issue find the courage to face it and look it in the eyes until the fear dissipates. Dealing with it head-on enables you to reap the benefits. To recognise your strength and courage rather than allowing it to fester unresolved.

Sometimes it may seem easier, when you notice that something is 'off' to shrug it off. In my experience asking the person involved and giving them the opportunity to be honest is a courageous move. Being willing to ask a question that you may not like the answer to and staying open-hearted and open-minded to the answer is a true strength. It balances intuition (yin) with action (yang). Even if the other person does not reciprocate, you have done yourself proud. The truth always comes to light in the end.

Male and Female Energy

John Gray in his book of the same name suggests that 'men are from Mars and women are from Venus'. The two energies of masculine and feminine are creative in different ways. Whilst you are healing, I'd encourage you to adopt the more feminine qualities of compassion, self-love and patience.

Whilst masculine energy tends to flow in straight lines, feminine energy moves in curves. Healing does not occur in straight lines; it is cyclical like a spiral curriculum. Masculine energy is best adopted when you need to take action.

Masculine energy is characterised by *doing* and achieving and is shaped through logic and reason. In modern society it's the energy that is encouraged, favoured and even expected. The feminine is intuitive, oriented towards receiving and allowing, and characterised by *being*. This is the energy that society is learning to embrace now that it is clear; stress and overwhelm have a negative impact on productivity and well-being. When these energies are balanced, you experience a greater sense of harmony and fulfilment.

Five Element Theory

The cyclic phases of yin and yang were developed into a theory called the Five Elements Theory by the Chinese Yellow Emperor in around 2600 BC. His deepening understanding of the energies of yin and yang motivated his writing of the classic work *Nei Ching*, the original book on Chinese Medicine.

Sometimes called the 5 Transformations, it is a dynamic philosophy for understanding the living world. The five elements are wood, fire, earth, metal and water. The theory is that everything in the universe is an outcome of change, and results from the movement of the five elements and their relationship to each other.

Nine Star Ki uses the foundational energies of yin and yang, feminine and masculine and the 5 Elements and divides them further into eight energies or phases positioned around a central point. The nine distinct energies are described by offering nine archetypes which will be explored in the coming chapters.

Knowing your personality archetype and remembering your strengths, especially in times of suffering can be empowering and uplifting. It can help you overcome struggles by reminding you to dig deep into your gifts and skills.

Patterns

Nine Star Ki is a beautiful blueprint that offers a way of connecting with who you are on a deeper level. To help you discern which habits and patterns in your life would benefit from greater equilibrium.

I have found it to be an amazingly accurate, practical and insightful tool to guide me, since I discovered it around 11 years ago. It is a gentle, loving and encouraging wisdom that is profound in its simplicity. Nine Star Ki delights by unearthing hidden treasures and perspectives that were just under the surface waiting for you to find.

The system for determining your archetypal patterns is based on your date of birth. Nine Star Ki teaches that every year of your life has a specific plan and purpose. Being aware of where you are currently positioned in your personal time map enables you to navigate your activities, energy and emotions and get the best out of them, like working smarter not harder.

Nine Star Ki is a nine-stage cycle. It can be used as a nine-year cycle, and/or a nine-month cycle. Within the cycle are nine personality archetypes. There are patterns and symbolism imprinted within each of the nine stages, from 1 Water to 9 Fire that you can connect to for deep personal insights and valuable messages to guide you. The archetypes help you to gain a deep appreciation and love for yourself and others. Coming to know yourself, your talents, gifts and purpose as well as your emotional landscape, patterns and challenges offers valuable insights. It enables you to be more confident in all that you are and all that you do.

When you know who you are and what you stand for it saves time and energy because you have a guideline to refer to. There is a theme for each year, a specific plan, meaning and purpose that brings focus to your life and offers detailed guidance for you to make the most progress each time. Each cycle has an emotional pattern associated with it that may influence your thoughts in unexpected ways. It is useful to be aware of these patterns ahead of time so that you can work with them instead of being confused or overwhelmed by them.

The more you can align with the energy of each stage of the cycle, the more easily life can flow. Each year is different to the year before and the year after, and so by understanding and immersing yourself in each year's theme you are building and strengthening the foundations for future years too.

Each of the nine archetypes is steeped in symbolism from nature. Patterns and imagery including family dynamics help you to connect with and relate to the essence of each one.

You are not alone. There is a, guiding, loving force in your life. You are connected to something bigger than you. There are purposeful invisible patterns in your life that when followed instil a sense of safety and reassurance. You have innate qualities and an energetic map to follow that can keep you from getting lost in the darkest times of change, loss and grief.

When you view life as presenting a loving force that is 'for you' and not 'against you', it will enable you to be braver, more creative and more secure in yourself.

Remember that feeling of everything being, OK? The sense of calm, peaceful, assuredness that comes over you in moments when you feel loved, safe and secure? This book will show you how to capture that feeling every single day.

Changing Energy

Life is so much better when you have a good level of connection with the truth of who you are and the flow of love that is all around you and available to you always. When you feel isolated or that you must face a situation alone with no support, everything seems harder, darker and scarier. With no outlet for your fear and stress a vicious cycle can form. When you are alone with your thoughts you can get immersed in stories that are not true and torture yourself unnecessarily. Easily getting fixated on perspectives that could be unkind, unloving and unhealthy.

When you connect to your true self, to other people and to the guidance around you, life takes on a vibrant buoyancy that you can track. You feel free to do what you want to do. There's no compulsion to check your phone or email every two minutes to find out what someone is doing or thinking. You can go ahead with your desired plans confidently without second-guessing yourself. You won't be so irritated or prickly with your loved ones and best of all know how to catch yourself when you feel stress rising.

They say change is as good as a rest. Although you may not be happy with the change you have endured, allow me to show you how reassuring it is to trust the process.

2

CYCLE OF CHANGE

A MENTOR ONCE TOLD ME THAT WE ALL HAVE OUR OWN GIFTS AND talents and that if we are interested in helping others to think about using those talents like being a driver on a bus route. Imagine you are a bus driver with one designated route, at each stop you pick people up and take them to their destination. Some people will stay a few stops with you, others just one or two.

Your route is just one aspect of the many journeys the passengers will embark on in their lives. Your role is deliver them skilfully and safely from A-B depending on your specialist route. As your route is one of many for the people you encounter, you don't have to get bogged down in taking on the responsibility of getting them to another point on their overall journey.

I intuitively knew early on in my separation that I was navigating the twists and turns of this tumultuous life initiation in ways that would also be invaluable to you. Many people commented on how gracefully and lovingly I was working through the experience and one day it dawned on me that not everyone has the tools to do the same should they wish to. I understood that my marriage was a few stops along my route and was not destined to be part of my whole journey. But did others?

People began to ask me if I had always felt guided in some way, what the secret was to the way I chose to circumnavigate this heartbreak? They commented on how they admired how I seemingly chose to pick myself up, dust myself off and concentrate on moving forward with my life unencumbered. That I chose love.

Reflecting on my journey from heartbreaking change to cultivating contentment, I was able to map out my journey using the cycle of Nine Star Ki as a lens. I saw how I progressed through each stage of this cycle of change and what self-soothing remedies I adopted to heal and ride the wave. It wasn't a linear process as healing doesn't occur in straight lines. Like nature healing is cyclic, for me it was a spiral, moving between the layers and coming back to thoughts, and feelings to perceive them in more loving, empowered ways. Always building, each layer on the next.

There are so many experiences in life that can cause grief, shock and heartbreak. The death of a loved one, divorce, the ending of a friendship, the loss of a job. All come with a set of emotions such as anger, dejection and anxiety.

Exploring your thoughts and emotions is vital for healing. To move through them picking up wisdom along the way. You will oscillate between different stages of learning and healing as time goes on. The adage 'life goes on', whilst seemingly flippant when you are suffering, is true. Life goes on and change is certain. Having a blueprint or map for navigating a cycle of change enables you to heal consciously and intentionally.

Nine Star Ki Map

This map illustrates the cycle of change and shows where each of the 9 archetypes sits in the mandala.

Mandalas are beautiful circular patterns that represent the Universe, completeness and self-unity. They can be used with inner reflection practices such as meditation which give you a sense of completeness and peace.

3

NINE STAR KI- YOUR GUIDING STARS

WHEN YOU WERE BORN THE WORLD WAS CONFIGURED IN A UNIQUE way. There was a specific energy in the atmosphere that you now carry as your constitution or archetype. On your birthday you were infused with the energy of the moment which shaped your personality, gifts, talents and the rhythm of your life.

Nine Star Ki is a map you can consult to help you heal, enhance self-awareness and plan so that you are in the flow of your life. It is like your love song to the world. When you know the tune, you can allow it to hum away to you in the background as a gentle guide and sing it loud and proud for all to hear and appreciate.

Your Nine Star Ki is comprised of 3 numbers; birth, heart and soul.

1st Number = Birth Star

Your optimal potential, your core energy; what drives you. To grow to your full potential often requires overcoming challenges and developing the strengths of this energy. This is your main energy that dances with the other two.

2nd Number = Heart/ Inner Star

Represents where you go in times of stress and is the seat of your emotions. It's the wounded aspect of the inner child. Being driven by this energy is like being in the passenger seat of life. Healing these wounds can bring tremendous freedom and empowerment.

3rd Number = Soul Star

This reflects how you do things in the world, how others often see you and indicates your hopes and aspirations. It is your Soul's highest evolution.

Using the Nine Star Ki Chart

Before you dive in and use the chart to discover your archetypes there's a couple of things you need to know.

★ Nine Star Ki is based on the solar calendar, a system built on the observed cycles of nature. Instead of a new year starting on 1st January, it begins on 4th February. This is because 4th February is the mid- point between the solstice on 21st December and the equinox on 21st March. Over the centuries it was thought to be the most natural starting point for the year.

What this means for you is that if your birthday falls between 1st January and 3rd February, that in Nine Star Ki you were born the previous year. For instance, if you were born on 1st January 1980, in this system you were born on 1st January 1979. Another example would be, if you were born on 3rd February 2000, in this system you were born in the previous year on 3rd February 1999.

When looking at the chart if you were born between 1st January and 3rd February, keep this in mind. It is only the year in these special circumstances that changes.

For any birthday between 4th February and 31st December, nothing changes and you do not need to do anything. If you were born on 10th October 1982, you were still born on 10th October 1982.

★ Until you reach 18 years old or 2 cycles of 9, you are mainly living in and influenced by your inner or heart number. Once you reach adulthood then you will adopt your birth star energy. This may be a smooth transition or may take some getting used to as you navigate the new you and all the gifts and strengths it comes with.

How to find your Birth Star

Let's now discover what your guiding stars are. Don't be scared you don't need to be good at maths. The numbers are used as a shorthand to the elements.

Your Birth Star is the main energy that governs and guides your personality and journey through life. It's the starting point for understanding your fundamental nature. As you are unique, the way the energy flows through your experiences will be individual as will the way you move through life.

Look at the chart below and find your year of birth. Then trace upwards until you find the corresponding birth star number between 1-9 which is a shorthand for your archetype.

For example:

If you were born in 1976 your birth number is 6

If you were born in 1980 your birth number is 2

If you were born in 1973 your birth number is 9

(Remembering that if you were born between 1ˢᵗ January and 3ʳᵈ February you have to go back one year.)

Nine Star Ki Chart- Years

9	8	7	6	5	4	3	2	1
1901	1902	1903	1904	1905	1906	1907	1908	1909
1910	1911	1912	1913	1914	1915	1916	1917	1918
1919	1920	1921	1922	1923	1924	1925	1926	1927
1928	1929	1930	1931	1932	1933	1934	1935	1936
1937	1938	1939	1940	1941	1942	1943	1944	1945
1946	1947	1948	1949	1950	1951	1952	1953	1954
1955	1956	1957	1958	1959	1960	1961	1962	1963
1964	1965	1966	1967	1968	1969	1970	1971	1972
1973	1974	1975	1976	1977	1978	1979	1980	1981
1982	1983	1984	1985	1986	1987	1988	1989	1990
1991	1992	1993	1994	1995	1996	1997	1998	1999
2000	2001	2002	2003	2004	2005	2006	2007	2008
2009	2010	2011	2012	2013	2014	2015	2016	2017
2018	2019	2020	2021	2022	2023	2024	2025	2026
2027	2028	2029	2030	2031	2032	2033	2034	2035

Nine Star Ki 81 Combinations

Now that you have your Birth Star which corresponds to your year of birth, you can find your complete Nine Star Ki, all 3 numbers. Firstly, find your birth number shown 9-1 across the chart. Then trace down and across the left-hand side and find where your day and month of birth fall.

For example:

If you were born on 6th March and your birth star is 4 then your 3 numbers are: 472

If you were born on 14th May and your birth star is 7 then your 3 numbers are: 757

If you were born on 28th January and your birth star is 1 then your 3 numbers are: 169

Nine Star Ki Chart

	9	8	7	6	5	4	3	2	1
Feb 4- March 5	959	822	784	656	528	481	353	225	187
March 6- April 5	941	813	775	647	519	472	344	216	178
April 6- May 5	932	894	766	638	591	463	335	297	169
May 6- June 5	923	885	757	629	582	454	326	288	151
June 6- July 7	914	876	748	611	573	445	317	279	142
July 8- Aug 7	995	867	739	692	564	436	398	261	133
Aug 8- Sept 7	986	858	721	683	555	427	389	252	124
Sept 8- Oct 8	977	849	712	674	546	418	371	243	115
Oct 9- Nov 7	968	831	793	665	537	499	362	234	196
Nov 8- Dec 7	959	822	784	656	528	481	353	225	187
Dec 8- Jan 5	941	813	775	647	519	472	344	216	178
Jan 6- Feb 3	932	894	766	638	591	463	335	297	169

Experience the energy

To get a good sense of your Guiding Stars let's take a tour, if you will through the seasons in your mind's eye. You will likely recall that winter is very different to summer and spring to autumn. That morning has a different energy from afternoon or evening. The seasons and cycles of time feel different, they have various qualities about them.

You hold all the elemental energies and qualities within you however your guiding stars are more prominent. Your principal guiding star or archetype has the biggest influence on you. It will be evident in your life in all sorts of ways from the type of furniture you buy to the sorts of activities you enjoy doing.

A way to experience the cyclical nature of the seasons and the distinct archetypes within Nine Star Ki, is to take your attention to your breath and practice noticing the rhythmical, cyclical nature of breathing.

Take 5 Pause and Practice

Take a moment to take a full breath, expanding your lungs. Experience the pause or transition from inhalation (breathing in) to exhalation (breathing out) and then exhale feeling your lungs and ribcage contract. Take some time to experience the sensations. Wait for the next inhalation to come by itself, no need to rush it.

Did you get a sense of everything rising as you took an inhalation? Your chest lifting upwards and your stomach expanding? Then that gentle pause, before your stomach started to slowly contract like letting air out of a balloon?

Inhalation, like the spring arrives, grows and builds until you get to the summer with that feeling of fullness at the end of the inhalation. And then as the breath goes out, experiencing that like autumn when things fall away, leaves fall, a contraction. And then at the end of the exhale, a quietness, stillness, a pause that is described as winter. Then out of that pause, springtime arrives and there is expansion through your lungs on the inhalation.

Breathing continues in the background without your attention.

The energy of your guiding stars behaves in the same way- it continues to support you in the background and now and then you will become mindful of its presence and will be able to seek and soak in its wisdom.

Each of the guiding stars in Nine Star Ki correspond to an element, season and time of day. To illustrate their characteristics, below is a brief description of each of them.

Water (1): Night, Winter

Water is the dark, quiet, potential and stillness of midnight and midwinter. It is reflection, prayer, meditation and sleep. People with this energy generally like to go with the flow, enjoy freedom, are intuitive and don't like too much structure.

Wood/Tree (3,4): Morning, Spring

Wood energy is active like the beginning of a new day and the upward energetic movement of sunrise. It is filled with enthusiasm, creativity and new possibilities. People with this energy tend to be influential, driven and direct, although they are also vulnerable to self-doubt and anger.

Fire (9): Summer, Noon

Like midday, Nine Fire is very active. It's the energy of peak summer where there's sunshine, parties and flowers in full bloom. It's the height of the midday sun as it illuminates our path. People with this energy are loving and passionate. Somewhat delicate and can wear their hearts on their sleeves.

Earth (2,5,8): Afternoon, Late Summer/ Early Autumn

Earth is the downward movement of the sun and the onset of autumn, also representing the transitional stage between the seasons of the year. People with Earth energy are nurturing, supportive and responsible. They give their resources freely and need to be sure to maintain good boundaries so that they are in service to others not servants.

Metal (6,7): Early Evening, Late Autumn

Metal is the inward, downward contracting movement of dusk and late autumn. Highly aware of details and have high expectations. Metal calls you to search for ways to refine your work and yourself. Metal people have an air of authority and are eager to help. Metal people can struggle with self-worth, they take their responsibilities very seriously.

The Nine Birth Stars

Your Birth Star

Whilst the following descriptions are detailed and give you a huge insight, Nine Star Ki as a full modality is much more in-depth. I've been a student and a practitioner of Nine Star Ki for over a decade, and I cannot distil all its magic in a few chapters. If you would like to know more, I do offer individual personalised readings which go into your full Nine Star Ki (all three numbers) in detail, visit www.guidedbylove.co.uk to connect with me and find out more.

1 Water Birth Star

Years

1900, 1909, 1918, 1927, 1936, 1945, 1954, 1963, 1972, 1981, 1990, 1999, 2008, 2017, 2026, 2035

Imagery

Water, iceberg, waterfall, well

Time of Day/ Season

Midnight, Winter, Solstice

Family Member

Middle Son

The middle son (in the middle, between the other two sons) is diplomatic, helpful and independent. Always looking for a win-win situation in family life and arguments. Potentially very much at ease with all members of the family through using the skill of reflecting back everyone's feelings.

Signature Strengths

Creative, innovative, easy-going, intuitive, diplomatic.

Catchphrase

Still waters run deep

Archetype

By observing and appreciating the qualities of water in nature, it is possible to connect with the qualities of the 1 Water personality.

1 Water energy is reflective, characteristic of contemplation, meditation and sleep. If 1 Water is your birth number, then your energy lends itself towards you being a deep thinker and from those depths come lots of ideas thus you have the capability of being an innovator. You take a philosophical view of life and are intuitive, sensitive and like to find meaning.

Water can be fresh, vital and active like mountain streams, appearing to be lively and positive with a spirit of adventure. At other times deep, brooding, slow and calm like ponds, lakes and the sea. You will display all 'colours' of the spectrum throughout your life at various times.

1 Water people have an independent nature which likes to explore. With the easy ability to find the way around obstacles in life, to see connections, and then consider objectively how to move them forward. Your ideas come from an inner knowing more than thinking.

1 Water's like to flow and enjoy freedom where possible and dislike being obstructed. You are not easily contained. You are therefore someone who values your own space and enjoys independence. With that space and depth, you have the opportunity to process emotions and experiences deep within you, this can sometimes take some time. If you tread water for too long, you may miss opportunities. Water also needs movement and flow otherwise it stagnates.

Like an iceberg there can be lots going on beneath the surface with your emotions that others cannot see. The hidden part of yourself, the part that holds your emotions deep inside can be easily hurt as people may not recognise how you are feeling. Being a strong and often quiet person, you may not divulge how much you have been hurt and it may come as a surprise if you share it later. You can be stubborn and withhold information as you think other people do the same. Remember that communication is important and aids the integrity and quality of all your relationships.

Whilst you require lots of time to 'be' and have quiet time, your 1 Water energy also benefits from guidance and direction. Most water sources have some sort of container or structure to follow like a riverbank or a teacup. Without containment you can be chaotic and undisciplined-think of a river bursting its banks!

Guidance comes to you from your ancestors, intuition and the fabric of life. You are connected to everyone and everything, to the unknown and mysterious. Allow yourself to get still enough to hear the guidance available to you.

Famous 1 Waters

Captain Cook, Diane Keaton, Andy Warhol, Helen Mirren, Cameron Diaz, Bob Geldof, Chris Evert.

2 Earth

Years

1899, 1908, 1917, 1926, 1935, 1944, 1953, 1962, 1971, 1980, 1989, 1998, 2007, 2015, 2024, 2034

Imagery

The Earth

Time of Day/ Season

Lunchtime/ early afternoon in late summer

Family Member

Mother

Mother energy is receptive, helpful, supportive, diplomatic and caring. The person you go to when you need a listening ear, a warm hug or something delicious to eat.

Signature Strengths

Deep thinker, reflective, philosophical, intuitive, diplomatic

Catchphrase

What can I get you to eat?

Archetype

2 Earth qualities are epitomised by the breastfeeding mother. The maternal energy that is caring, steady and reliable.

2 Earth energy is like lunchtime; a time for discussion, people with

this energy are interested in other people's well-being and so will talk to others and ask questions to find out how they can be of assistance.

If 2 Earth is your birth number, you will naturally be good at finding out what's going on and what needs to be done. You are great at organising and are exceptionally kind and thoughtful. You will work away in the background to get things done. You'll be the one at the end of the party washing the plates and helping to tidy and clean up. You shine in a position of service although you are not a natural-born leader.

2 Earth energy is the quality of unconditional giving, symbolised by the Earth who gives you all her natural resources so that you can thrive. Family, friends and relationships are most important to you. 2 Earth folks are the peacemakers, incredibly loyal and patient.

Caregiving and mothering are a primal quality of life. In our modern-day society, it has been exploited and not honoured in the way it should be. Be aware of constantly giving your resources and carve out plenty of time for self-care. Give from the 'overfill 'of your cup rather than giving away your last drops of energy to other people. If you are stressed or unbalanced it can lead to feelings of martyrdom, resentment, being overlooked and a lack of boundaries.

You can find it difficult to receive so do watch out for overworking and being over-serious or compulsive. Do ask for what you need and want in a way that others understand clearly- i.e., be specific.

A frequent emotion for you is worried. This comes from the archetypal mother who wants to ensure her brood are all taken care of. This tendency does not serve you well as the worries tend to repeat and spin in your head. When you catch yourself worrying imagine yourself literally stepping out of the 'spin' to gain clarity and focus.

Famous 2 Earths

J F Kennedy, Marilyn Monroe, Michael Douglas, Daniel Radcliffe, Pablo Picasso, The Dalai Lama, Louise L Hay.

3 Tree

Years

1898, 1907, 1916, 1925, 1934, 1943, 1952, 1961, 1970, 1979, 1988, 1997, 2006, 2015, 2024, 2033

Time of Day/ Season

Dawn or Sunrise / early spring

Imagery

Thunder, shoots breaking through concrete

Family Member

Eldest Son

The first-born son can explore, discover and try out things for the first time. An action taker and ground-breaker. Whether male or female, the Eldest Son is investigating what life has to offer for his future siblings.

Signature Strengths

Action taker, optimistic, spontaneous, independent, visionary

Catchphrase

I'm getting on with it

Archetype

Imagine a new little shoot so excited and determined to be alive that it pushes its way through concrete. This is the energy of 3 Tree. As a 3 Tree, you are usually bursting full of ideas and creative expression.

3 Tree is the vital energy of early spring and early morning. Imagine sunrise, when the birds are singing, a new day full of possibilities is beginning and enthusiasm fills the air with a sense of childhood effervescence.

Your energy is impulsive and creative. It is an initiating, doing energy, that will likely have you bubbling with projects. Your drive is strong which can make you competitive. You have a warrior-like energy, strong, fierce and ready to act. You value doing over being.

Like the image of thousands of baby sea turtles clambering their way to the sea, or young shoots being squashed- not all your ideas will survive and come to fruition. You are fearless about trying new things and embracing your creativity. It doesn't matter if a creation doesn't work out, you fail fast and try again. If frustration turns to anger, you can be like thunder- boom and then it's out of your system and over!

3 Tree energy is quite vulnerable, especially when the spirit of effervescence is oppressed. Life has a way of stifling you at times. When you have a plan, you like to action it and if it doesn't materialise or go efficiently it can be incredibly frustrating for you. Whilst you value your independence it's OK now and then to seek the support of others.

In conversations you tend to like directness and don't enjoy long discussions about a problem. You want to 'cut to the chase', figure out what's wrong then fix it. You can enjoy challenging others in interactions turning conversations into debates that you like to win. Be mindful that this style of interaction can be perceived as pushy or aggressive which may need to be softened with other personalities.

Sometimes 3 Tree energy can lead to self-stagnation through overthinking or mentally generated stalemate. The antidote to this is to physically move- dance, play a sport, go for a run.

Famous 3 Trees

Barack Obama, Robin Williams, Charlie Chaplin, Vincent Van Gough, Frank Bruno, Gabrielle Bernstein, Kyle Gray.

4 Tree

Years

1897, 1906, 1915, 1924, 1933, 1942, 1951, 1960, 1969, 1978, 1987, 1996, 2005, 2014, 2023, 2032

Imagery

The wind, trees, bamboo

Time of day/ Season

Late spring and late morning

Family Member

Eldest Daughter

The first-born daughter is always searching for new ways to express her creativity and work. Typically expected to look after the parents in older age, she may sometimes feel a sense of disappointment, like she has missed out on all that life has to offer. She can give guidance and inspiration to her younger sisters.

Signature Strengths

Tender, adaptable, practical, thoughtful, reliable, great common sense, conversation

Catchphrase

I'm not sure about that

Archetype

4 Tree energy is like a gentle wind- easy-going, gentle and open-minded. Like the wind you can be very adaptable and resourceful- changing directions as needed. If you allow yourself to bend like bamboo and be flexible, you can be an ingenuous creator. You have a great capacity for vision and can be ahead of the times. However, you don't tend to plan too far ahead, preferring to take things step by step and enjoy surrendering to the present moment.

You have a charming approach to life and are incredibly tender and kind. To others you may appear to be lucky- this comes from being in the flow of life. When you are fully connected and available to grace things naturally come to you. 4 Tree energy can be beautifully utilised as the 'wind at someone's back' supporting and gently guiding. This energy lends itself well to coaching, mentoring, counselling and being a good friend.

Be cautious not to overanalyse, overthink, stagnate or give in to self-doubt as adaptability out of balance can lead to overwhelm and procrastination. Fear of judgment can make it difficult for you to ask for help and be over-guarding of your feelings- remember people love to help and support you so do reach out. Friends will be only too happy to help and will not think you are complaining! Don't isolate yourself. If you need an outlet-talk to someone.

You like to feel in charge and in your power and so when others shame, belittle or cut you down, you hate it. This treatment can make you feel small, silenced and dimmed. Remedy this by accepting that not everyone thinks about or perceives things in the same way and love your individual uniqueness.

Just like plants break through the soil, 4 Tree people are the ones who create breakthroughs in old, outdated ways of being. You have a natural creative drive that needs to be directed into something positive- a task or cause that can benefit humankind otherwise you can get restless.

You are likely to challenge the status quo or question unnecessary rules and will use your creativity to find alternative routes and solutions. If your progress is blocked, then your emotional response is anger. This can look like being too hard on yourself although you'll be more upset if you think someone else is putting obstacles in your way. The negative version of anger is destruction. The healthy version is drive- use anger like a booster rocket!

Famous 4 Trees

William Shakespeare, Galileo, Martin Scorsese, Usher, James Corden, Nicole Scherzinger, Katie Holmes.

5 Earth

Years

1896, 1905, 1914, 1923, 1932, 1941, 1950, 1959, 1968, 1977, 1986, 1995, 2004, 2013, 2022, 2031

Imagery

The central point, a wheel, an earthen bowl and Ying Yang symbol

Time of day/ Season

The pause between seasons

Family Member

Part of the family and yet relatively distant from the other members. Takes on the qualities of all the other eight stars.

Signature Strengths

Leadership, guidance, catalyst for healing and change, bold, great at systems/ analytical

Catchphrase

What's the strategy?

Archetype

5 Earth is the centre, a catalyst, all energies touch it, and it touches all other energies. It is a very strong supportive energy. Think of being 'centred' or having a reference point or place to come back to when life's challenges and emotions pull you off balance. The centre is the place you know you have to come back to.

If you are a 5 Earth, then you are a powerful force of nature. An image of this energy is a wheel. It is the hub, like in the centre of a turning wheel, people often look to you for leadership and guidance. You can help 'turn things around' for them. You are resilient, resourceful and a natural problem solver. 5 Earth people have a very stabilising energy and tend to be practical, organised and have lots of common sense. With extraordinary problem-solving abilities, you can come up with solutions for individuals and groups making order out of chaos.

Being outside the 'family', gives you a tendency to learn from life outside the family, from your own difficulties and experiences. Sometimes situations can be extreme, involving success and failure. You can bounce back from life's ups and downs and have great resilience.

Like a toddler experiencing the world, you wander round like a mini sumo wrestler, wide-eyed, curious and determined. The strength in a toddler's belly and gait makes them resilient and centred. They will not be held back in their explorations and will bounce back from discoveries that were painful or frightening.

5 Earth is a powerful and grounded energy. Your heart knows how to ground and centre you so that you can be a catalyst to move through challenges. Your presence is likely to stir change in others. You may notice that at times people around you are not ready to receive your natural 'stirring' quality, you will know by their response to you. Your presence can create an intensity. This is wonderful when people light up with new ideas and are well received (usually they won't know why- they'll just have a sense that being around you facilitates awareness). It can be disarmingly uncomfortable if they are not willing to change in some way and so unfortunately you may find yourself at the sharp end of the stick.

You are often in the centre of things and people are naturally drawn to you. Community and connection are very important to you. Seek out people who recognise and welcome your energy, that welcome your insights. Spend less time with people who drain you or do not raise you up.

31

You are at your most contented and balanced when you are being of help to others and being recognised for your efforts and achievements. You are endlessly caring and will show up as a strong support for others. You are the solid ground beneath our feet and a source of healing and nourishment.

A lack of acknowledgement for your contributions coupled with movement from all angles can make you unsure of your place in the world and can lead to self-doubt. Thus, you have a strong longing to find a place or a niche for yourself. Be sure to use your gifts for yourself too as a lack of self-care and awareness can make you complain, be impatient and blunt. Remember that no matter what else is going on around you that you are loved, and you are the most important person in your life.

Famous 5 Earths

Mahatma Gandhi, Sir Walter Raleigh, Henri Matisse, Richard Attenborough, Albert Einstein, Usain Bolt, Millie Bobby Brown.

6 Metal

Years

1895, 1904, 1913, 1922, 1931, 1940, 1949, 1958, 1967, 1976, 1985, 1994, 2003, 2012, 2021, 2030

Imagery

Father, Heaven and sword

Time of Day/ Season

Evening in late autumn

Family Member

Father

A father takes responsibility for the family and are known for their fair dealing of situations. Whether you are a male or female 6 Metal you will come across as straightforward with a natural air of authority. Sometimes the wish for fairness and rationality can appear too rigid.

Signature Strengths

Natural leader, authority, loyal, moral, direct, noble, rational, wise

Catchphrase

I know what you need to do.

Archetype

Metal is associated with autumn- the leaves are turning red and yellow and are falling off the trees, the weather is becoming crisper, and the daylight becomes shorter. All around there is a process of letting go, exhaling and eliminating what is no longer needed, making space to inhale inspiration.

6 Metal carries a powerful energy, symbolised by the divine father. Father energy is loving and respectful and as such people listen to you. There is no 'if', 'but' or 'maybe' with this archetype. You tend to think that you are right and especially about what others need to do. This energy is sharp and focused like a horse with blinders on.

You are a natural leader and have a strong sense of justice. You prefer to give advice, rather than take it. 6 Metal is a protective energy that can be strong, authoritative, precise and practical. Family is very important to you, and you are the most loyal of all the archetypes. You use your wisdom and wit like the edge of a sword to cut through the extraneous and get to the heart of the matter. Accuracy activated by wisdom and tenderness.

You have a creative energy that enables you to initiate/ activate projects and then complete them with precision and discernment. With a capacity to focus you get things done!

Clarity comes down from the energy of 'heaven' into your crown which shows up as a strong intuition. Metal has the ability to accrue wisdom and make decisions and refinements. This energy brings everything together in a melting pot and alchemises it into gold, impurities being cast away.

Any process where you are seeking answers or higher knowledge is a very metal activity. In the forefront of your mind are big questions like 'What is life all about?' With the ability to access deep equanimity, to be quiet and centred at your core and embodying the power of divine light, expressed through the heart you can use your intuitive gifts to serve others in a beautiful way.

The ability to be calm and clear can be overlooked by yourself and others due to society's tendency to encourage doing, doing, doing. The prevalence of just keep doing enables the voice in your head to frequently suggest that you are not good enough which drives you to do more, often leading to self-criticism. Think of a stereotypical family father and his need to provide. Holding this energy expresses as a tendency to feel a tremendous sense of duty and responsibility.

Now that you have an awareness of this tendency, you can recognise it and use your sword to prune what no longer serves you such as harsh, critical and cutting self-talk and replace it with a warmth and sweetness to soften that edge.

Famous 6 Metals

William Wordsworth, Captain Scott, Desmond Tutu, Madonna, Wayne Dyer, Justin Bieber, Reece Witherspoon.

7 Metal

Years

1894, 1903, 1912, 1921, 1930, 1939, 1948, 1957, 1966, 1975, 1984, 1993, 2002, 2011, 2020, 2029

Imagery

A still lake and jewellery

Time of Day/ Season

Evening in autumn

Family Member

Youngest daughter

The youngest daughter brings all the experience that coming into the family last can provide. A carefree spirit arising from the secure knowledge other more responsible older siblings will take care of the details and worry. A reflective quality shines through with a youngest daughter, in spiritual, emotional as well as in amusing ways.

Spectrum

Fun loving, outgoing, receptive, good listener, charismatic and graceful

Catchphrase

Isn't that beautiful?

Archetype

If your birth number is 7 Metal, you are in tune with the lighter side of life. You are all about fun, being sociable and relaxation. Your days are filled with accomplishing beautiful things with grace. Your energy is associated with sunset, autumn and reaping the rewards of the harvest. A time of accomplishment and the joy of success whilst celebrating with friends and family.

7 Metal energy is focussed on achieving beauty, people with this energy see beauty in all things and they inspire us. You have a wonderful touch in art and music/sound and exhibit an instinctive sense of how to make a space gorgeous.

You like things to look good including yourself and so you are likely to have a wardrobe filled with lovely clothes. You take care of yourself physically by exercising and having self-care treatments such as massages or facials.

Like the element metal, you are very good at reflecting the qualities of the environment and telling others what they need to hear, this is symbolised by the lake. You notice the energy around you, the vibes and essence of what people say and don't say. Rather than sharing your observations openly you will often take what you have learnt and decide how you can best utilise it for yourself. For example, if you notice a parent behaving badly, you won't necessarily call them out, instead you will vow not to behave in such a way yourself as you have recognised the unhealthy pattern.

It can take you quite a bit of time to reveal how you truly feel as you are deeply private. You tend to worry about being good enough and can be overanalytical and perfectionistic. Your focussed energy can be stubborn at times, and you can go into denial, trying to keep the surface of that lake smooth and perfect. As you are so good at reading others, you require space and alone time, a chance just to be yourself. People close to you will need to recognise the signs of brooding and gently nudge you to open up and express your emotions.

When you have a good balance of inner and outer reflection time, you can be charming, quick-witted and make a great host. You have a flair for communication and expressing yourself. You can make people smile and laugh which is a good talent to have.

Famous 7 Metals

Sir Isaac Newton, Sean Connery, Iris Johansson, David Beckham, Katie Winslet, Angelina Jolie, will.i.am.

8 Earth

Years

1893, 1902, 1911, 1920, 1929, 1938, 1947, 1956, 1965, 1974, 1983, 1992
2001, 2010, 2019, 2028

Symbolism

Mountain with a cave

Family Member

Youngest Son

The youngest son has had the benefit of observing and taking onboard everybody else's dramas and triumphs. He has had the opportunity for reflection and is therefore very good at expressing the accumulation of knowledge, particularly in an intellectual way.

Signature Strengths

Strong, stable, persistent, composed, contemplation, strong sense of justice and fairness.

Catchphrase

Is this fair?

Archetype

8 Earth is the time between deep winter and spring when the seeds underground are coming alive. The seeds of change are within you and as such you have a revolutionary energy. You use this strength to support change. In nature the image for 8 Earth is the mountain. Mountains are strong, immovable and you can lean on them. Mountains also tend to support all sorts of life on their slopes. 8 Earth people take

their responsibilities very seriously. They are hardworking, reliable and steadfast in the face of difficulty.

By holding the strength of a mountain, life will give you opportunities to use this gift, so that you can recognise it. Therefore, you can take on or are handed difficult challenges and responsibilities in life. You did not come to coast you came to transform like a butterfly. Your primary energy is the ultimate space holder for the transformation and evolution of your own and other people's lives. You have a deep nurturing quality and will go to great lengths to support others, often when no one else will.

Taking the analogy of the mountain further, you are firmly planted in the Earth and so do not move quickly. You tend to move through life methodically, intentionally and with purpose. You have a slow and meticulous attention to detail which you can get lost in and can frustrate some! It can sometimes seem that nothing is being done however your action deepens rather than spreads- you delve down into what you want to pursue.

Getting too bogged down in the details instead of reviewing the big picture can result in feelings of confusion and not being able to prioritise. The remedy to that is reaching out to others for encouragement and suggested ways to take action so you can get your feet back on the ground.

Within the mountain is a cave. As your emotions are linked with mountain energy it is important that you spend time in your cave, in silence and contemplation to receive wisdom and listen to your innermost thoughts and guidance. A cave could be your car, a den, or a space in your house that's quiet that you can be alone when needed. Without this time, you can become stubborn and uncommunicative and a caller at your cave could get a surprise with the sharp end of your tongue. In a clear and grounded state, you are skilled at using your accumulated knowledge and sharing it i.e., teaching others to discover their own buried treasure.

Famous 8 Earths

Beatrix Potter, Arnold Schwarzenegger, Elton John, Stephen Spielberg, Chris Hemsworth, Amy Winehouse, J.K. Rowling.

9 Fire

Years

1892, 1901, 1910, 1919, 1928, 1937, 1946, 1955, 1964, 1973, 1982, 1991, 2000, 2009, 2018, 2027

Symbolism

Fire (from a flame to a forest fire) and the heart

Family Member

Middle Daughter

Streetwise, expressive and sparky, when you meet a 9 Fire you will not forget them easily. The middle daughter can shed light quickly on the problem at hand, with a laser focus she will come to conclusions and help those around her see what is obvious. This challenging and direct nature can be dazzling.

Signature Strengths

Inspiring, outgoing, passionate, warm, strong, heart-centred, expressive, active.

Catchphrase

Let's spread some love

Archetype

9 Fire is the energy of midsummer and noon, a peak time for activity. A vibrant, active energy that encompasses all the qualities of the sun. It is bright, rapid expansion and full speed ahead.

9 fire people are full of passion, charismatic and social. They burn brightly and are usually easily noticed, although some may be quieter. They are open-hearted, outgoing and thoughtful. They express and spread love and joy. They are affectionate and have a sweetness about them.

If you are a Nine Fire you can burn brightly for all to see when you express yourself fully. With a highly creative mind, activity and variety are important to you. You are a quick learner and have a constant drive for accomplishment and fulfilment. Acknowledgement from others can motivate you so be sure to say so if you need 'stoking'.

You lift people's spirits up, are charming and fun. You are gifted with making others feel happy and inspired. The phrase "Oh that looks like fun" will be a regular part of your vocabulary!

You are a busy person who generally has lots of balls in the air. You can manage your projects effectively by working on them in short bursts. Fire drops away to ash and goes still as part of its process so a healthy 9 Fire will schedule rest to be balanced and content.

Cultivating your relationship with Fire will assist you to become more self-aware and utilise your strengths. Some questions that you can ask yourself as a 'check-in' are:

- ★ Do I need the energy of home fires (heart, passion, compassion)?
- ★ Do I need the focus of a candle flame?
- ★ Am I being catastrophic in my thinking?

Out of balance you can tend towards catastrophic thinking and/or chaotic behaviour. You may lash out or think 'It's all gone to hell'. When you witness this within yourself bring it back and contain it by paring back your activities. Think of this pattern as a forest fire that started as a spark and then spread out of control.

Nines also tend to have a vulnerable heart and you may easily find yourself being emotional around someone who is upset. This is because you are an empath and so easily relate to and feel the anguish of other people. Be mindful of your own energetic boundaries and ensure that you are not absorbing too much of other people's energy mistaking it for your own. Remember that not every thought or feeling is yours when you are in close proximity or thinking about someone else.

Whilst it's lovely to be supportive of others, it is very draining on your energy to process emotions that aren't yours.

Due to your vulnerable heart if you experience betrayal, hurt or loss please don't allow it to close your heart. Your strength is to spread love, to offer affection and connection. If you close down not to feel pain, you will also close off your capacity for joy and happiness too.

Famous Nine Fires

Jane Austen, Walt Disney, Martin Luther King, David Bowie, Kate Moss, J.R.R. Tolkien, Paula Radcliffe.

How Nine Star Ki helped my healing journey

Since I discovered it, Nine Star Ki has helped me to be present and mindful of my thoughts and actions. This spiritual practice was incredibly helpful during my heartbreak journey and continues to support me now. It enabled me to understand myself better and where I was situated in my personal time-map which acted like a guiding light during my darkest days.

Knowing my Nine Star Ki pattern which is 4.1.8, and choosing to use it as a measure against my responses enabled me to be less reactive and overwhelmed. It was a handy reminder that I am driven, adaptable and gentle, yet prone to self-doubt. That I am a helpful person, a deep thinker who always looks for a win-win in a situation and yet prone to being consumed by fear. And that I am strong and nurturing yet pre-dispositioned towards stubbornness.

Being aware of my strengths enabled me to tap into them, to turn them up, like using an equaliser to manage my emotions on particularly hard days. Recognising when I was slipping into the challenging aspects of my personality helped me to take a step back rather than being overcome and governed by my heightened emotions.

My 4 Tree energy has helped me to be flexible in my thinking, to consider other people's perspectives, to be kind to myself and to focus on a way into and through my pain. I was able to recognise when I was holding onto disappointment and the negative impact that had on my ability to let go. To notice when I acted as the 'wind at someone's back' far longer than was healthy for me and to stop and take care of myself instead.

My 1 Water energy has aided me to 'go with the flow' of life, to recognise that there will always be obstacles and to avoid stagnating by finding ways to float downstream. Trying to fight against the current is fruitless and tiring! 1 Water energy helped me to dive deep into the source of my thoughts and feelings so I could emerge back up on the surface with fresh perspectives. There were also times when my intuition whispered to me (even shouted; loudly), and I resisted the truth until I dared to accept the necessity for change.

My 8 Earth energy enables me to be self-reflective, accumulate knowledge and have the strength of a mountain. To nurture myself and those around me. There were times though when I was resistant to reaching out to others for support, feeling that I 'should' show my best face and not let anyone know the pain I was in, to hide it deep inside the mountain cave. I got stuck and bogged down instead of looking out from the mountaintop to see the bigger picture.

My break-up also occurred at the beginning of a new Nine Star Ki year, a 4 year in my 9-year cycle. The fact that it happened then, suggested to me, that this life-changing shift was to become the central focus of the year. The Nine Star Ki years will be further explained a little later in the book. But for now (to give you some context) a 4 Year is all about change and rapid growth followed by a 5 Year which is all about healing.

Knowing that I was immersed in the energy of change allowed me to gradually soften into acceptance. Life was letting me know that it was time, it was meant to be. That the energies of my personal time map had aligned for my rapid growth of which my marriage was a casualty. This information gave me comfort and peace, something to hold onto and focus on. Along with the knowledge that subsequent years would offer healing, reaping the benefits of change and growth and finding joy.

Take 5 Pause and Practice

Now that you know what your Birth Star's natural strengths and qualities are, I invite you to reflect on where and when you notice these patterns appearing in your daily life. Intend to notice how the energy guides your movements, behaviours and feelings. Sometimes the energy can be subtle like a soft breeze and other times you will recognise it with the clarity of a lightning rod.

4

MAYA'S STORY

As the logistics of the seismic change ahead of me started to bombard my head, thoughts spun round like a spinning top and every now and then a clear question would pop out. What about the dogs?

It felt like time was of the essence because he was packing up to go so, I thundered quickly downstairs and found him sorting clothes out in the den. Iris had caught up with me and we stood in the doorway of the kitchen and den. I asked in a direct yet slightly panicked tone "What about Maya? What about the dogs? Do you want me to look after them?"

Maya was his dog, a gift from me several years before. After he had been on a trip with friends and their Patterdale, he had waxed lyrical about them. I was driving along a lovely country road not long after the trip and a thought popped into my head, "Wouldn't it be great to get him a Patterdale puppy". I was initially surprised by that out-of-the-blue thought, however as I drove along, a feeling of excitement started to rise within me. Anticipation began to bubble up from my tummy to my heart, a warm fizzy sensation that erupted into all sorts of thoughts and plans.

It's doable, my mind suggested with a smile arriving on my face. Yes, it is a good time. I am working part-time now so there would be someone around, and the puppy would get plenty of attention and not be left alone for long periods. We could go for more walks as a family, and he would be over the moon. I imagined seeing my husband's delighted face and that filled me with joy. I loved to see him happy, and the bonus would be all the benefits to the whole family.

I hatched a plan to get a puppy for his birthday later that year. I trawled the internet for advice and information on the breed and where to look for a reputable breeder. I even did all the research covertly on my phone using a different search engine to the one on our shared computer. I had discovered not long before, by way of a playful comment 'Ah I know what you've been doing today' that he could easily see what I had been looking at on our home computer. I felt so proud of myself for creating such a special surprise for him.

I found a breeder I was happy with and so the day came to meet the puppies for the first time. I was thrilled that we were the first people to meet them so would have the whole litter to choose from. The breeder had asked if we would want a boy or girl, tan or black and so I let him know it was a surprise and entirely my husband's choice.

I took him over to the breeder's house on the pretence that we were picking up a washing machine for my Mum. I could barely contain my excitement and I thought he would surely suss that something was amiss as I couldn't hide it! As the breeder opened the front door and we heard the dogs barking, I turned to him and said, "We're not really here for Mum, we're here for you. Go through and choose one". With a slightly confused look on his face, he went inside the house. Once he saw the puppies and realised what was going on, he looked over at me and said "Really?" with a big smile on his face.

He focussed on Maya straight away; it was love at first sight. He went straight to her and picked her up gently, "Hello you" he said with a sparkle in his eye, and I knew instantly that she would be the one we would take home.

Now standing in the doorway, he looked up at us and said, "I'm not taking her with me, she can just be rehomed."

Iris and I stared at him in utter disbelief. And then we both screamed at him.

Iris said clearly shaken and very upset "You can't say that she is meant to be your dog, how can you say that?"

She couldn't believe what she was hearing, what her dad was saying. Later she told me how much that moment had upset her and how confusing it was. She felt like he was being heartless and was so angry with him that she wanted to punch him.

I was shocked, disbelieving and enraged when those words came out of his mouth. Perhaps said in the heat of the moment, whilst trying to escape from our questions and yet he had uttered them. My head couldn't wrap around the idea that he could so easily abandon, potentially give away a beautiful being that he apparently loved. I was furious that he could even think that way.

I understand now that part of my anger was fear. Fearful that if he could treat his beloved dog that way then it wasn't too much of a stretch to give the same treatment to myself and the kids. To abandon us. To throw us away.

Maya stayed with us of course along with her beautiful son Pepper. She laid on the bottom stair next to the front door for weeks, alternating looking out of the window for her dad to come back. She barely ate and she was very subdued. When I looked into her eyes, I could see how sad and dejected she felt. Pepper was clingy and needed a lot more reassurance and since then he has been very sensitive to raised voices. They were both as heartbroken as we were.

5

CYCLE OF LOVE MAP

THE CYCLE OF LOVE MAP IS INTENDED TO SET THE SCENE FOR THE coming chapters. To give you context for how being guided by love works with Nine Star Ki and the practices contained within the book.

The fundamental premise of the model is:

> **Love is a process that involves action, expression and intimacy.**
>
> **You are whole, perfect and loved.**
>
> **Life's distractions can make you forget this. There are tools and practices that remind you of the truth of who you are.**

Love is a verb, it's an action word. Love is a process that requires expression, effort and application. It is a cyclical process that deepens with time and experience. Love is a process you can learn and build on to understand what you need to thrive in a relationship- with yourself and others. To journey through lust, infatuation and love to find true love and true intimacy. The more you can move through the process consciously and intentionally the deeper the learning and greater the result.

On your journey through life so many things can veil the truth of who you are. Throughout this adventure called Life remember please that you are loved beyond measure, that you have so much to offer the world by simply being yourself and that you are fundamentally OK. Through utilising the tools and practices within this book you will rediscover how loved, cherished and supported you are. How strong and courageous you can be and the inner resources you can draw upon when needed. You now have a toolbox to serve as a reminder of your awesomeness.

The Cycle of Love Map model offers 6 guidelines and is illustrated by a fruit tree. A tree represents strength. Just like you, they can stand tall. Trees grow up and outwards representing how a person grows stronger and increases their knowledge through experiences throughout their lifetime.

1. Soil- You are made of love; you go back to love, and in the middle (throughout your life), you can choose love. Love is your foundation. Just like soil, love provides nutrients, nurtures and supports.

2. Roots- You are born with a set of energies that are described through the Nine Star Ki which inform your personality/ archetypes and influence what you do, say and think. Your roots also include family heritage and genetics.

3. Trunk- You have life experiences and are given certain messages from caregivers that form your beliefs and values. This forms your core, where you get your strength from. Recognising and observing unhealthy patterns in your family and deciding to heal them so they will end with you, is a powerful and courageous gift to all.

4. Branches are the extensions of how you live, how you reach out to people, and how you connect. Are you honest, brave and ask for what you want and need? Or do you shy away and avoid intimacy and connection? Has life taught you that you are

amazing, encouraging you to reach for the sky and follow your dreams or are there areas of self-doubt and deprecation?

5. Fruit- What you harvest from those intentions, choices and actions. Is your fruit juicy and succulent or is it bitter? Is your life; your mindset, home and work in alignment with your true self? Are you where you want to be? What comes out of you when you are squeezed, when you are stressed? Do you recognise it and choose self-compassion, or do you spurt out anger and frustration?

6. You can rise above instilled belief patterns and reach for the sky. Connect to the Universal energy of love. All you must do is choose it and then take guided action steps.

If you take a slice of a tree, you can see how it grew and under what conditions it lived in. You can also take an inventory of your life and look for how you have grown, what conditions you have lived in and how the conditions need to change for you to thrive.

Take 5 Pause and Journal

Take a moment here to consider the following questions and write down your answers. Perhaps find a cosy corner, slip off your shoes and have a delicious drink to savour whilst you're here.

- What nurtures and nourishes you?
- Is it necessary to trim some branches, clear mental and physical clutter?
- What changes need to be made in your life to produce delicious fruit?

Life gives us opportunities to set intentions and make choices from either love or fear.

Love is an action

Love is a choice

It takes bravery and vulnerability to choose love and self-love. It is hugely rewarding to reach for the sky and to place yourself firmly rooted in the centre of your universe. To soak up everything that nurtures you first so that you can grow strong and then produce fruit that can provide sustenance to others.

Part 2

DISCOVER AND GO WITHIN

6

CONTRACTION

ONE OF THE MOST PROFOUND WAYS TO UNDERSTAND YOURSELF AT your core is to experience a contraction in life. An experience that rocks your foundations and perceptions so much that you have no choice but to surrender to the change. To open your mind and heart to the lessons life is offering to you. To surrender and fall back into the supportive arms of the love around you and inside you.

Contractions in life tend to be painful, excruciating even at times and can make you feel small and demoralised. You can feel like the wind has been taken out of your sails and you are stranded out to sea without hope of rescue. However, just like contractions in labour, the ultimate prize is new life. The hardest part of birth is towards the end, just before the baby arrives and women often feel like they can't go on, that they have hit a wall. It's common for women to say they can't do it; they have run out of energy and the pain is too much. Yet moments later when they are holding their baby in their arms, there is a rush of love and pride. The pain all worth it and the memory of the birth all but forgotten.

I remember as clear as day the joy and pride I had when my children were placed on my chest after giving birth. Looking down at them with awe and love. Mesmerised at the perfect beings I had the privilege of growing and bringing into the world. I felt so amazed at what I was able to create.

Contractions always lead to expansion. Pausing to learn what they are teaching you is a beautiful gift to self and will ripple out to everyone around you.

Disconnection

Disconnection is extremely painful, especially when you have been deeply connected to someone or something and it is taken away. It can feel like a dark, lonely and isolated place, with little light at the end of the tunnel.

When I first felt the pain of disconnection, the enormity of what it meant to be separated landed with full force in my mind and body like a blunt trauma from a sledgehammer. I reeled under the realisation that I was no longer part of us. My mind went into overdrive, into complete panic. It was flooded with thoughts of "What am I going to do?" and "What ifs?".

It felt unbearable. I didn't know what to do with myself, I wanted to run away, escape, for it all to be a bad dream. I remember lying on my sofa, my heart pounding so hard and rapidly it felt like it would come out of my chest. It had never thumped so violently before, and it scared me.

"You'll be OK, a friendly, calm voice, echoed in my head. You're having a panic attack, the worst thing that will happen is you will faint and wake up again. Just lay down and breathe."

My body was telling me in no uncertain terms how panicked she was. Then worried that the kids may be distressed at seeing me like this, I pulled a blanket up close to my face and snuggled it. Pleading with my body and mind to relax.

I placed one hand on top of the other on my panic-stricken, thumping, broken heart and took some deep breaths. The warmth of my hands felt soothing and nurturing and whilst breathing deeply and gently I finally dropped off to sleep.

Disconnection is painful because there is a sense that something is missing, that something has been lost. With that comes a sense of yearning and grief. When feeling disconnected often the smallest of actions to further cut ties can cause distress, emotional and physical pain and anguish. Particularly in relationships where you were connected with so many threads that held meaning and memories. When they are severed it can feel like a piece of your heart has been ripped out.

I remember the pain and grief of realising that I would never again experience things that were specific to us that I had grown so accustomed to. Our 'us' was gone. I would have to cook all my own meals, drive myself and the kids everywhere we needed to go, take the dogs for a walk without the catch-ups or the male voice of authority that they responded to.

Ultimately it was the loss of my family unit that was the hardest to bare. The romantic notion of walking down the street holding hands when we were old and wrinkly vanished, sharing the joy of our future grandchildren together, gone, and the wider family parties that would no longer be possible, or at least in the same way.

I had to let myself feel the pain of each layer of disconnection and all that went with it such as feeling disappointed, sad and trapped. The emotions came in waves over time, not all at once. With each layer came more acceptance, space and peace.

It took me a while to realise that through wanting so badly to save my marriage, I had taken my attention and focus completely away from myself. I searched for ways to fix, repair and prove. I bought book after book around relationships, listened to podcasts, soaked up short courses and yet nothing helped. In fact, the space between us got bigger and bigger. The more I tried, the more I was met with silence and resistance.

Although I had learned a lot about relationships and how to cultivate more love, intimacy and connection, these months had shown me all the ways they were missing. Eventually I was able to throw away my rose-tinted glasses.

I realised how important emotional connection was to me. I discovered that no matter how much we are bonded to others, it is vitally important that connection to ourselves is nurtured first and foremost. It was like a light was turned on in my head, having been in a dark room searching for the switch. I could see clearly the necessity to pause and explore who I was and wanted to be- my values, needs and non-negotiables before I moved forward.

There are patterns that you can fall into when feeling disconnected, harbouring in the hope that they may serve as a remedy to reconnect. Unfortunately, these ways of attempting to close the gap can often make the space cavernous instead.

Recognising the following 9 ways of approaching challenging situations when you slip into them, can help you to identify whether you are inward or outward focused. Or to put it another way whether you are connected to the truth of who you are and making decisions from that place or are more focused on attempting to change an outcome or person and therefore disconnecting from yourself.

7

9 UNHELPFUL WAYS TO RECONNECT

Feel free to read the numbers that you most identify with first and then circle back to the others. There are lots of juicy thoughts here that you can drink up and digest.

1. Fixing

2. Forcing

3. Control

4. No one is coming to save you

5. Needing answers

6. Negative thinking

7. Staying stuck

8. Expectation

9. Lack of love

1. Fixing

You simply cannot fix other people and most especially when they do not want or ask for your help. Whilst being able to "see" someone's wounds can be helpful to understand them on a deeper level, it is necessary to be cautious about turning that knowledge into only focusing on their potential. It is not your responsibility to fix them. You may find that you are starving yourself in the process.

Everyone has their own path to follow and will flow through life at their own pace. When someone appears to be suffering, it's human nature to want to help. To take the pain away. You can encourage and guide however people must come to their own conclusions, to learn their own lessons.

People are naturally encouraged to adapt or grow throughout life by different situations and experiences and it's your job to trust that process. No matter how frustrating or hard it is.

If you find yourself wanting to fix or save someone it's likely time to consider the toll it is having on you.

Allow me to illustrate this point through a story from my experience. It happened a few months after my husband had moved out, when I was still clinging to the tiniest thread of hope that we could reconnect.

After I had gone round and dropped off the food parcel, I was on alert.

My friend Emma said, "What the hell were you thinking?"

The question made me squirm in my seat as clarity rose within me.

Initially pleased with myself for my 'good deed', I felt light and hopeful with a spring in my step.

Then the doubt creeped in.

Every ten minutes I was checking my phone for a 'thank you'.

Later, as I lay in the dark, I couldn't settle.

A whole stream of thoughts running through my mind.

I thought I'd created an opportunity to connect, to show my affection, in the hope I could begin to fix what was broken and yet I was now reeling from the self-made repercussions.

Where was the thank you? My hands, stomach and head tensed up in frustration.

Thoughts whirled....

Now came the anxious despair, washing over me like a wave- the sinking, heavy sensation filled my chest.

A quiet despondent voice spoke...

It's not coming, is it?

And what's worse, it won't be coming ever again.

Tears pricked my eyes, and the knots in my stomach turned to fluttering butterflies from anxiety.

Darkness wrapped around me tighter.

And then came the anger, at myself, at him, at the whole sorry situation.

How rude not to acknowledge my gesture, how heartless, how...

I vowed to myself in that moment to put myself first. To feel the pain of separation and disconnection and to prioritise healing and connecting with myself. To do something kind for me instead.

Kindness to myself now looks like checking into my inner guidance first and asking

"Who am I doing this for and what is the intention behind it?"

For example, for a few years I have been loyal to two local raw food suppliers for our dog food. I wanted to share my custom with them and so went back and forth, on alternate weeks, often going out of my way so that I would be 'fair' about spreading out my custom. One day I caught myself fretting about running out and neither of my usual options was convenient. I realised that there must be an easier way to get what I needed without putting myself out so I bulk ordered what I needed and got a monthly delivery. The relief and novelty when my first delivery came was wonderful.

When you feel a compulsion, a yearning to 'make' something happen, you have been pulled off-centre. Pulled by threads of desperation, overwhelm and not knowing what to do. This can lead to rash decisions cloaked as solutions. Be sure to check in with yourself to ensure that the solutions you choose are truly in alignment with who you are and what you want. The ones that feel light and easy in your body.

Take 5 Pause and Practice

Take a moment here to close your eyes and take some long deep breaths. Feel your body relaxing. There is nothing to do except to simply be here with your breath.

Place one or two hands (one on top of the other) on your heart and continue to breathe slowly.

What sensations do you notice?

Do you have a sense of urgency? Breathe into it. Allow it to flow through you and take its natural course. It will subside into a sense of calm.

Keep breathing. Continue to invite calm.

Wait and breathe.

Then from this place of balance, consider your next step.

2. No Forcing

When you would really like something to happen, there can be a danger of attempting to force something or someone into submission. Wanting something badly can cause you to be impatient and act impulsively. Tension can build and may erupt in unhealthy ways like driving too fast and behaving negatively towards innocent people. The more you force the more likelihood that there will be damage, breakages or pain. Attempting to force your will onto something drains your energy and can prevent you from allowing the wonderful things that are available to you to come into your life.

Forcing can lead to resentment, bitterness or martyrdom. It can be disempowering to fixate on one specific outcome and does little to serve your purpose.

A mantra or saying that really stuck with me and helped a lot throughout my healing process is: 'It is what it is'.

It is what it is.

Meaning that sometimes a situation cannot be changed and so must be accepted. It is not giving in to defeat as that could be disempowering. Instead, it is loosening your grip, relaxing and allowing.

I came across a practical joke called the Chinese Finger trap when the kids got them in their party bags once. It is a great metaphor for a problem that can be overcome by relaxing and not trying too hard to solve it. The finger trap is a simple puzzle that traps the person's fingers, often the index fingers in both ends of a small cylinder woven from bamboo. The typical initial reaction is to pull and try to force the fingers out, but this only tightens the trap. The way to escape the trap is to push the ends toward the middle, which enlarges the openings and frees the fingers.

When the mantra 'It is what it is', popped into my mind, it was as if true love stood up and said enough is enough, I am going to make myself known to you so you can break free from this illusion and stop trying so hard. To guide you back to your centre.

What a gift.

It took some time; it took acceptance and courage.

I realised that when it comes to true healthy love sometimes it's not clear what to look for when you haven't had the principles modelled to you. It can be quite easy to fall into accepting negative behaviours despite the niggles and red flags because you see potential. It can then be quite a feat to stop trying to hold onto and influence your version of that person. To see past the potential, no matter how well-meaning it may be.

True, wholehearted, pure love requires no force. It feels calm and grounded. It brings the best out of you and supports you to be yourself.

Take 5 Pause and Practice

Repeat the Mantra

It is what it is

It is what it is

It is what it is

Each time you say it feel the strength that arises within you. The first time you say it, there is likely to be no sense of conviction. Once the truth of the words fully rings within you and resonates in your mind and body, the more conviction there will be behind them and the more belief you will have for them.

Notice what happens in your body.

Is there a softening? A letting go?

Notice your thoughts.

Does the tone and quality of your thoughts change?

3. No Controlling

Having self-control can be helpful when directed towards something positive you wish to achieve for yourself. Yet attempting to control others has a different quality, it erodes confidence and can make you and others feel small. Having control may seem like a tempting option to get what you want, however adopting a domineering or aggressive stance will create distance rather than connection.

Control does not feel very pleasant, and the result is likely to be rebellion from the person it is aimed at. I certainly felt that way one day when I was getting on with daily life and was suddenly faced with an unexpected correspondence.

The house was bustling with activity, the kids milling around chatting and Pepper, our dog excitedly dropping his favourite squeaky toy at my feet. He looked up at me with hopeful eyes suggesting that I would stop preparing lunch and play.

I looked down at his eager face and smiled, feeling happily content with the scene around me. A thought washed over me around how much I love family life and how blessed I am to have my children and fur babies close.

The squeaky toy hurtled down the kitchen to Pepper's delight as my attention was suddenly averted due to a familiar ping from my phone. It was a new email, so I curiously sat down at my laptop to read it and as the words came into view my heart sank, the playfulness drained away. It was like a tap turned straight onto full, the force of the water plunging downwards with vigour hard, fast and loud.

My eyes felt like they'd been stabbed with a red-hot poker at what they were being subjected to, my heart grew heavy, and my stomach knotted, my whole body sank and slumped into the chair. I sat dumbfounded with my head in my hands, gripping my hair at the content of the correspondence. Waves of fear and defiance washed over me, with a clear thought 'I will not be controlled.'

I wanted to pick up the phone and let him know how unfair and downright ridiculous I thought he was being. How could he be asking for monthly reports on the kids from me because they had chosen not to speak to him- they're adults for crying out loud! Is he unaware of how the divorce process works? Thoughts screamed in my head and made me feel dizzy.

I eventually softened by reminding myself to "just breathe". Bringing awareness to my breath and consciously taking some deeper inhalations and exhalations. Allowing my shoulders to gently melt down and observing the rest of my body relaxing like the domino effect.

My heart went from racing to calm and my mind from whirring to settled as I realised that I was in resistance mode and having difficulty accepting what I was faced with. I know when I am resisting something because I feel frustrated and tense. My shoulders find their way close to my ears and my jaw aches from clenching. I shook off the frustration like a dog expelling water from its coat, and understood that I was resisting viewing this from a compassionate and loving place.

I understood, painful as it was, that the behaviours and actions that I had grown accustomed to when he was in love with me, were very different now. As shocked and disappointed as I was that things had changed so radically, I knew it was still my responsibility how I responded.

One of my favourite mantras popped into my head,

'I make healthy choices from a place of love'

These words are written on a card on my desk, and I see them every day. If I ever get stuck in a thought or emotion that isn't healthy for me, or I want to move forward with an action or decision and I am confused, it almost blinks at me like a neon sign. It makes me smile and reading the words instantly connects me to my heart. From the warm, loving and tender space of my heart, I am encouraged to look again at how I can choose to respond from a place of love.

I shut my laptop, took some long deep releasing breaths and made some space for the subtle loving voice of my intuition to purr away in the background until I knew what to do next.

Take 5 Pause and Practice

Recognising Resistance, Preference and Control

Take a few minutes and drop into the questions below. Allow any answers to arise naturally, without actively thinking or analysing the question:

What am I experiencing now?

How would I like it to be different?

Disliking what is happening and wanting what isn't here is a form of resistance, which can become a preference and then eventually control.

Honestly consider how you habitually react to this scenario and be curious about the gap between what is happening and how you would like it to be different. Can you bring some gentleness into the gap? Can you release your grip and allow for new perspectives and options to appear?

4. No one is coming to save you

As a child you rely on other people to protect you and so as an adult when your inner child is afraid, you expect and hope for an outside source of help to come and rescue you when needed. To take away the pain or solve the situation. Whilst outside sources of help such as friends and family are important additions, as an adult, no one is coming to save you, except yourself.

Whilst this may feel harsh and bruising in the moment of realisation, like you have been abandoned in the cold, it truly is beautifully empowering. You can resist it, wish it was different, wallow in self-pity and perhaps even stamp your feet. Yet when you come to understand that you are in the driving seat of your life and allow your creative mind to search for solutions, you experience the full benefits of change and can take full credit for your healing and actions moving forward.

In the early days of being separated, I fantasised about situations in which he would come and rescue me, realise what a terrible mistake he had made and resolve to make everything better. Of course, that wasn't helpful thinking, I just wanted to connect with him. It took me a while to accept that my life had changed irrevocably. I still expected that I could somehow encourage him to reciprocate my love and kindness.

Things started to break around the house, the vacuum cleaner stopped working, the kitchen light tripped a fuse, and a tap began to drip uncontrollably. For the first time in decades, it was up to me to sort these issues out. At first, I felt quite alone, vulnerable and sorry for myself. It turned out however, to be an opportunity for me to put my big girl pants on and reach out for help. All I needed to do was ask.

Our lovely neighbour quickly and easily resolved the vacuum issue and my wonderful dad sorted everything else. I felt accomplished, supported and safe. I knew then that I wasn't alone, that I am never alone and that there is always love and support around when needed or asked for. My dad and I had fun looking at kitchen taps and deciding which one would be best and then when he came to fit it, I was able to witness beautiful moments between my dad and my son Alfie.

Dad was awaiting a replacement knee operation and although fully competent to do the job, Alfie recognised that his Granddad would benefit from his help. "Let me do that Granddad" Alfie said, referring to climbing under the sink, as a lovely smile grew on my dad's face. This kind of opportunity for bonding had not occurred between them before. Alfie contorted his body under the sink whilst being passed various tools, granddad looking on guiding and explaining what he needed to do. It was such a lovely moment for me and one of the glimpses of light that kept me going in the early days of my grief.

Take 5 Pause and Journal

Write down all the things that you need help with.

How do you feel about asking for help? What thoughts, beliefs and body sensations arise when you consider asking?

What skills do the people in your family and wider circle have?

What do you know you could do if you gave it a go?

Now look again at your list and decide what you are going to tackle yourself and who you are going to reach out to for help and support.

For example, I discovered that it was easy enough for me to mow the grass, take the rubbish to the tip and do some painting.

People love to help, let them.

5. Needing answers

All the answers you seek are within you.

Searching for answers outside of yourself, rather than trusting what you think and feel gives your power away. I knew on the morning of my anniversary that something was deeply wrong. Rather than greeting me in bed with our usual morning cuppa, I found my husband downstairs fully clothed with his own cup of tea. I tried to make light of it but I understood this act had ominous intentions and ramifications.

Sometimes you will not get the answers you seek or the sense of closure you desire, in the form of reasons from others. In those situations, you need to carry on with your life with an open heart.

In stressful situations its normal to be emotional and not to be in a neutral, logical frame of mind. Your brain will search for any answers it can find to get you back into a state of equilibrium. The answers your brain adopts or suggests may not be true or accurate. Have you ever looked at an object ahead of you, can't quite make it out and then settled on deciding it is a particular thing, only to get closer to it and realise that you were mistaken. Like looking out to sea and mistaking buoys bobbing up and down for seals?

It's like looking at an abstract painting. You can search for hidden meanings and yet at the end of the day, it may well just be random loops of colour.

Even when you or someone else believes that there is justification for a certain behaviour, often it's a perspective of the moment and it may not hold true when in a balanced state of mind. Like an impulse buy at a shop on a whim, at first you must have it and then when you get home you realise that it's not needed or is unsuitable.

When something happens that pushes you to start seeing clearly, it is uncomfortable because no one likes to be disillusioned. It takes courage to determine whether you are in a fantasy and if you are not being honest. You want to believe something different; to justify it, to make it fit your model of being OK so that nothing must change. Your work is to recognise the reality. To understand what is fantasy and where you are pretending that it's OK when it's not.

You are not responsible for anyone else's behaviour or problems; people will behave and act how they choose to. You have no control over this. It's tough yet true.

After an awkward breakfast on my wedding anniversary, I asked my husband if he had anything planned, imagining something romantic like a woodland walk and picnic. There was nothing planned, another red flag, and so eventually he suggested we go for a drive. He took me to a rural country shopping centre where there was a café, a small woodland walk and a complimentary therapy centre that he had wanted to go into to discuss his business opportunities.

We got out of the car and headed for the woods, I felt completely unloved and disconnected from him as he marched ahead with me trailing behind. Trudging through the mud and navigating discarded tree branches, I had the view of his back ahead of me. All the while I was hoping he would turn around, offer his hand and offer a warm smile. After a wander around the shops and before we had what was to be our final cuppa and cake socially as a married couple, he took me into the complimentary therapy shop and made plans to rent a room for his business.

"When someone shows you their true colours, don't try and paint a different picture."

-Unknown

A common thing that happens in the grief process is that you search for answers and when you cannot get the answers from the person you think holds them, you start to look to yourself instead. Unfortunately, when looking inwards in these circumstances all you will find are negative thoughts and beliefs. You may even blame yourself unnecessarily. Your inner critic comes out in full force and gnaws away at you like a dog with a bone.

For me the resounding question was "What's so wrong with me?", which after some time and self-compassionate inquiry I could answer. Nothing.

The evening of my wedding anniversary continued to be a surreal living nightmare. Fleeing the house to find some sort of solace, I found myself alone in my car, bewildered and scared from the treacherous stormy conditions. I knew it wasn't safe to drive, even to my Mum's so I went back and resolved to talk to him, to attempt to understand where this bombshell had come from. I went upstairs and found him in bed.

I stood rooted to the floor at the end of the bed and looked at him. The face looking back at me seemed almost made of stone.

No smile, no warmth, just a glazed stare.

I was confused, shocked, and taken aback by this sudden change in demeanour.

What had happened to the soft, gentle eyes? Where had the reassuring, knowing smile gone?

My mind raced, trying to make some sense of this.

My stomach in knots, heat rising to my cheeks, my heart ached with sorrow and sank slowly into a deep dark hole of despair.

Reaching for some sort of connection, I pleaded for some answers. I kept asking and asking, falling further into despair as silence boomed in my ears.

He rolled over, turned the light off and closed his eyes.

It was over.

He was done.

Dumfounded, unable to move or comprehend the enormity of this gesture, I just stood, for what seemed like an eternity. I eventually walked out of the room and shut the door.

I can still see and feel the shock and disbelief of how such warmth had turned into frosty cold. I didn't recognise him anymore- it was frightening.

Take 5 Pause and Journal

Consider the situation you would like to get some fresh insights on and write down all the facts, look at them objectively, like presenting a report.

What do you absolutely know to be true?

What is fact and what is fantasy?

What are their actions telling you (not their words)?

Hold yourself with compassion if the veil of illusion comes down, it can be extremely sad to be faced with the truth. Allow yourself to grieve the version you held onto.

6. Negative thinking

Blaming, criticising and making excuses are examples of negative thinking and prevent us from taking self-responsibility. A wonderful mentor of mine and communication expert Cynthia Kane taught me that the way you talk to yourself dictates how you see the world. And that if you talk in an unkind or unhelpful way then you will view your day-to-day experiences through this same lens.

> *"You must take personal responsibility. You cannot change the circumstances, the seasons or the wind, but you can change yourself."*

> -Jim Rohn

I got a lovely job in a local leisure centre a few months after my separation. Working in a customer-facing role is a wonderful way to observe people, their attitudes and behaviours especially during times of disappointment. There was a private party taking place in Soft Play one Friday afternoon which meant that members of the public could not gain entry for a couple of hours. One dad and his young daughter came in and asked to go into soft play and I let them know that there was a party and that they could come back later. The dad calmly acknowledged this information, looked down at his excited daughter and gently explained the situation. After a moment of disappointment, the daughter took hold of her dad's hand and quietly walked out.

Not long afterwards a lady and her young son came in. Again, I smiled as they came up to the desk and relayed the same information when she asked for place in soft play. However, this interaction was entirely different, the shift in energy palpable.

This lady's frustration exploded from nowhere and she angrily said that this was stupid, that other places allowed entry even when a party was going on. She spun around and with the same angry and frustrated tone, sharply told her young son that he wasn't allowed to go into soft play.

When he started to cry, she yanked his arm, pulling him away saying it wasn't her fault and that he should blame us as it was our fault.

I felt quite honoured that Life had clearly demonstrated right in front of me the difference our thoughts can make in a situation. Of course, I couldn't see into the minds of these families however their outward response indicated some definite differences.

The man seemingly had a positive dialogue playing in his mind. Perhaps something like, 'Oh well it would have been nice to go in, however, a child having a lovely birthday with friends and we can come back.'

On the other hand, the lady seemed to have more of a negative dialogue playing in her head. Perhaps something like 'I'm not allowed to just let my son play, why does there have to be stupid rules? I have just as much right as anyone else. It's their fault that my son is now unhappy'.

One of my all-time favourite stories to illustrate this point further is The Tale of the Two Wolves. It's said to be an old Cherokee parable.

The Two Wolves

An old Cherokee Indian chief was teaching his grandson about life.

He said, *"A fight is going on inside me,"* he told the young boy, *"A fight between two wolves."*

The Dark one is evil - he is anger, envy, sorrow, regret, greed, arrogance, self-pity, guilt, resentment, inferiority, lies, false pride, superiority, and ego."

He continued, *"The Light Wolf is good – he is joy, peace, love, hope, serenity, humility, kindness, benevolence, empathy, generosity, truth, compassion, and faith. The same fight is going on inside you grandson…and inside of everyone else"*

The grandson pondered this for a moment and then asked, *"Grandfather, which wolf will win?"*

The old Cherokee smiled and simply said, *"The one you feed"*.

Every day you make choices and these small, yet important choices define you. They are a statement of who you choose to be in this life, and what impact you will have on the world around you.

Whilst it may seem easier to feed the Dark wolf; to procrastinate, complain, dismiss, ignore, and give up. There is little effort in choosing these, yes perhaps some instant gratification and yet no personal growth.

The Light wolf is very different; it's harder to feed. It can be challenging, tiring and time-consuming to do things like learning, teaching, inspiring, sharing or abiding to new behaviours. These things take energy, effort, vulnerability and bravery. They take more time, and you don't usually see immediate results, they involve investment and patience.

The story continues...

The old Cherokee replied, *"If you feed them right, they both win."* and the story goes on:

"You see, if I only choose to feed the Light wolf, the Dark wolf will be hiding around every corner waiting for me to become distracted or weak and jump to get the attention he craves. He will always be angry and will always fight the Light wolf."

"But if I acknowledge him, he is happy, and the light wolf is happy, and we all win. For the dark wolf has many qualities — tenacity, courage, fearlessness, strong-willed and great strategic thinking—that I have need of at times. These are the very things the light wolf lacks. But the light wolf has compassion, caring, strength and the ability to recognise what is in the best interest of all."

"You see, son, the light wolf needs the dark wolf at his side. To feed only one would starve the other and they will become uncontrollable. To feed and care for both means they will serve you well and do nothing that is not a part of something greater, something good, something of life."

"Feed them both and there will be no more internal struggle for your attention. And when there is no battle inside, you can listen to the voices of deeper knowing that will guide you in choosing what is right in every circumstance."

"Peace, my son, is the Cherokee mission in life. A man or a woman who has peace inside has everything. A man or a woman who is pulled apart by the war inside him or her has nothing."

"How you choose to interact with the opposing forces within you will determine your life. Starve one or the other or guide them both."

My separation and heartbreak enabled me to practice the lesson of the Two Wolves, daily. There were days, even weeks where I fluctuated between self-pity, fury, confusion and grief. I was so frustrated with myself that I still cared and yet felt so hurt. I eventually learnt that you can hold conflicting feelings within you and keep them in balance like two sides of one coin.

It is possible to recognise feelings and not be pulled off-centre or weighed down by either the negative or positive. Allow them both to have space to be heard and then put them down. Ultimately, I learnt that you can love someone, care about them or hold them in regard and not agree with their behaviours. Thus, you have the choice as to how much or little of your time or energy to give to them.

7. Staying Stuck

When you have a shock, the body knows instantly and it activates the flight, fright, freeze response, however the mind can take quite a lot longer to catch up. It takes time to assimilate what has happened and to make sense of it. This gap can be a gift to help you adjust to change. There then comes a time when you need to let go.

My daughter Iris described this feeling as being 'on pause', like she was going through the motions of life and yet her emotions were held in suspended animation. She asked me to take her out to dinner one night nearly a year after her dad left as she wanted to talk. She told me that the pause button had been released and realisations and questions were popping up like popping candy.

What she shared was so familiar to me and yet hearing it from her fresh insight was hard to hear. It was like all the pain and realisation I experienced quite instantly a year ago was being replayed through my beautiful, kind daughter. Her words made my heart sink like a stone as she relayed her fears and disappointments. *"I'm never going to live with him or see him every day again, am I?" "Birthdays, Christmas and parties are going to be different."*

Listening to her share was like reliving all my realisations. Like a pebble dropping into my awareness had touched my emotions and eventually rippled out to touch hers. It also filled me with such pride that she had processed her emotions and was now coming out the other side.

I described to her my way of understanding our different paces of processing by using a simile. I said, *"For me, when dad told me he was leaving it was like a big heavy bookshelf full of books containing knowledge crashing down around me, some books hitting me, the pain and understanding of the ramifications instantaneous".*

I continued, *"For you, I see it like the books on the bookshelf have been sliding off slowly over time. Landing on the floor open to a page for you to explore and understand. Now your insights are coming at a quicker pace with the books flying off the shelf".*

I consider myself to be lucky. Lucky that I had some tools to process my emotions. At the start of my separation my thoughts and actions were worlds apart from where I am now. Looking back, I understand that I was in a process of unravelling and transformation. A necessary part of my growth and healing. I look back with compassion and as they say hindsight is a wonderful thing.

My early strategy to hold onto my marriage was to give my husband time and space. I gave myself a deadline, to give him an opportunity to reconsider. For him to discover that in fact the grass isn't greener and that it's greener where you water it, which in my mind was at home with us. Then I extended that deadline when I reasoned to myself that he just wasn't quite ready. His actions were telling me the truth and yet when he visited, he would tell me he wasn't sure if it was all over which gave me false hope. My friends could see the truth of the situation and yet I needed to come to that conclusion on my own.

Giving people extended time, more chances, attempting to show them more love, more patience or understanding can keep you stuck. If you find yourself making excuses for them, for their actions and choices you may well be stuck. People must take responsibility for themselves; you cannot do that for them.

Getting defensive if others attempt to widen your perspective, in my experience is another indication that you are living under an illusion and avoiding moving forwards. It is a fear response, that the status quo has changed, and the rabbit won't go back into the hat.

Holding onto someone or the promise of something is alluring and can be admirable, however eventually sticking to your guns becomes more painful than accepting the necessity to move on. The truth is, life without flow is not life: it is stagnation, where nothing can thrive.

Attempting to control a situation is not healthy. It keeps you stuck as you are not considering the possibilities of a beautiful future and instead fixating on something you do not have the power to change.

The only thing we have true agency over is ourselves.

People do show you their true colours, their true priorities and what they want to do through their actions. If though, you are wearing rose-tinted glasses, those colours can be distorted and confused. Taking off the glasses and looking at the actions of a person in the light of day can be illuminating.

If you have remained 'stuck' for a while, you can choose to get 'unstuck'. It's often just a shift in perception that will create a positive change.

Here are a few to consider:

You have yet to develop your Guiding Star reference point

If you are used to other people making choices and decisions for you, it's likely that you are not fully in touch with your own essence. If you try and make decisions based on what you believe is expected of you without knowing your unique desires, needs and qualities you won't be able to thrive. Going through life without a clear purpose or sense of direction is confusing and exhausting. It can make you feel apathetic, debilitated and hopeless especially when you cannot rely on certain people anymore.

Developing your Guiding Star reference point, helps you to focus on what matters to you most and make decisions that feel true and joyful to you. By developing an awareness of who you really are and what you want, you can keep on track with your new life's desires and goals. It is only possible to feel in alignment with yourself when you put your attention on what really matters to *you*, and you are able to self-validate your decisions.

I did this by asking myself how I knew when I had made good decisions for myself and how they felt in my body. I also wrote down my values, skills, dreams and desires. Together the answers from this self-inquiry formed my Guiding Star reference point. Now whenever I need to make a decision and I have some doubt, I can return to these points as a personal guideline.

Your body needs to feel safe

When you are feeling stuck, adding more pleasure to your life is highly beneficial. Pleasure is what the body feels when it perceives safety, connection, nourishment and healing. It is not only an emotion or a feeling. It is a physiological process that increases your immune defences, balances your hormones, and calms your nervous system. Mentally, it increases your capacity to learn and to find solutions to your problems, your self-esteem and your capacity to bond with others.

Adding pleasure and joy to your days will help you to feel re-energised, capable and inspired. When you feel good about yourself, your creativity increases, and your passion ignites. My go-to pleasures, to name a few are; being in nature, playing with the dogs, dancing around the kitchen, a luxurious soak in the bath, a delicious meal and beautiful flowers.

You're scared of being alone or of the unknown

It could be that you have been in a relationship for such a long time that you don't know how to be comfortable being alone. The thought of the unknown- life outside of the relationship is so daunting that you stay stuck in fantasising or wishing for a reconnection. This is a precarious mindset to have as it makes you vulnerable to going back to unhealthy patterns and missing out on beautiful future opportunities.

Being in your own space without any distractions can feel like a breath of fresh air. Treat it not as a time of loneliness, but instead an opportunity to explore your inner joy. Learn to be comfortable in your own skin, in your own company before inviting others in.

At first, I was scared of the unknown, all sorts of thoughts popped into my head. Would I be truly happy again? Would I have to travel to my ideal holiday destinations alone and would I be able to achieve my dreams and goals without a partner? Then I began to notice that I enjoyed the more relaxed atmosphere around the house, the freedom of doing what I wanted, when I wanted. I could watch whatever was on TV or Netflix that interested me without checking with someone else. I could relax and read books rather than jumping up to fit into another person's schedule. A new confidence arose within me that whispered at first, then exclaimed joyfully that I can create my life and shape it into whatever I want it to be.

Take 5 Pause and Act

Create a comfortable, cosy and safe space in your home and give yourself a 'Self Connection date'. You could light some candles, burn some incense, get your favourite food and drink and snuggle up to a good book. Take the opportunity to appreciate having time all to yourself. Notice that it can be very enjoyable to do whatever it is you want to do, including having full say over the TV remote!

For emotions that are stuck, watch a sad movie or play sad songs. Allow your tears to release pent up feelings. Let them flow freely to cleanse and renew, leaving you with a lovely sense of spaciousness.

8. Expectation

"Watering artificial flowers will never make them grow.
Stop pouring your energy into one-sided relationships."

-John Mark Green

Human beings do not like the feeling of being disillusioned or disappointed and so attempt to reduce the tension by changing beliefs or the source of information to fit the experience. This helps you to feel better and less uncomfortable with a situation that is desirable but is out of reach or out of your hands. The psychological term for this is cognitive dissonance.

When you are married, you expect the marriage to last, you expect to be loved and cherished. It is therefore natural to attempt to reduce the anxiety of potential loss by telling yourself that there is hope. You start to hope and then cling to the hope that things will improve, to expect that they will get better if you keep trying. You find ways to justify bad behaviour, give it an explanation so that you can reconcile it and therefore live with it. There may be a 'backstory' of emotional or physical abuse and so you may justify and rationalise their behaviours because there is a reason for it and accommodate them under the circumstances.

You may tell yourself things like "If I try harder to show them my love, then they will realise how much they are cared for and will stay/ try As well." "Maybe I'm asking for too much." "They didn't really gaslight me, they weren't thinking because they were rushing to get to an appointment."

If like me, you are empathic, you are also likely to have high expectations for yourself borne out of a need to please. Empathic people learn how to listen deeply so that they can be prepared for what other people around them may do, a type of self-preservation technique. You not only listen to words but to the use of words, the tone of them, the body movements and the eye contact that go with them. You can interpret silence and hear everything that people don't say.

This pattern, whilst being very beautiful in other circumstances, entrenches you in perpetuating 'trying' and 'fixing' and can plague you with confusion. Once you have earned more money, lost weight or kept the house spotless, you find that the goalposts have been moved further away. Calling this out is OK and yet may be scary.

Along with the expectation and hope, is an underlying fear. Fear that there will never be someone better or that you will be alone forever without a partner. This fear is an old pattern, stemming from previous conditioning such as having authoritarian parents, experiencing abuse or lack of emotional support when you were young. Somewhere along the line you got the message that you had to be 'good' or 'pleasing' to receive love. This belief then drives you to work harder, justify and explain away, sadly against your otherwise better judgement and intuition.

Managing expectations can protect you.

People do not tend to change. Once you are aware that the person you hoped they were is an illusion and that they are not amenable to change, managing your expectations is a healthy way to move on. Remembering that in a one-sided or unhealthy relationship they are unlikely to take self-responsibility, recognise that they are hurting you or want to learn how to emotionally connect. This knowledge sets you free. The truth will set you free, even if it is uncomfortable or bitterly disappointing.

Check-in with yourself and ask:

Is your kindness a choice or is it a trauma response?

Are your people-pleasing tendencies leaving you tending to people who give you the bare minimum? Are you giving them your fullest attention with the hopeful expectation that it will be reciprocated?

Is your wish to believe you are a 'happy family' blinding you from the truth?

9. Lack of Love

Love is a beautiful energy that flows like water. If allowed to flow unimpeded it can be life-giving, refreshing and cleansing. When faced with obstacles it can navigate them with relative ease, finding the smallest of cracks to flow through. However, when love is blocked it can damn up inside you.

Love is always a part of you. It is not something you lose; it is something you can choose to withhold. With no way to flow, water can stagnate, turning it from fresh to pungent. The love that is withheld from you (and others) becomes the pain and apathy you carry around with you. A good way to resolve this is to reoxygenate the water in the form of new ideas, experiences and perceptions. To practice open-heartedness, self-love and self-compassion.

Self-worth is a large part of love. Self-worth is the inner sense of being good enough. Worthy of love and belonging. It's about truly valuing yourself. When you continue to stay in a situation where someone is disrespecting you, you are being challenged to invest in yourself. Right now.

When you take responsibility for your situation, you can do something about it. This is the way to get empowered. If you make the problem about someone else, which is outside of your control, you don't have the leverage, the power to change.

"I don't love you anymore", are hard words to hear, probably the most heart-wrenching words that anyone can say to another person. Whether used in a way to be intentionally hurtful or honestly yet carelessly, those words hurt, a lot.

When these words were uttered to me, it knocked the stuffing out of me and because I'm human I took them to heart. I believed them. Not only that, I also took those words and made a meal out of them, I took them out for dinner and entertained them. "I don't love you anymore", was plated up and tasted like I'm flawed, I'm unlovable, I've done something wrong.

I went to town to attempt to figure out what had caused this dramatic shift, with the spotlight resolutely focused on me. At first my approach was self-deprecating, judgemental and blaming. I searched for all the ways I was at fault. Later I was able to gain a balanced perspective. In many ways taking responsibility for your part in any situation is empowering, importantly though it needs to be explored from a place of self-worth, compassion and acceptance.

As a tender and loving person, I chose to stand in my truth and to do the best I could to mirror love despite it not being reciprocated. I hoped that I could show that love can conquer all. What I didn't realise then was that it does. The difference is where you choose to focus that love. I was focussing love outwards to someone who no longer wanted to receive it whilst neglecting the most important person- me.

Love is an energy and energy cannot be destroyed. It simply changes form.

You can still show love towards someone and dislike their behaviour.

You can still show love towards someone and hold your boundaries.

You can still show love towards someone and let them go with grace.

My invitation is for you to take this as your opportunity to value yourself way more than you already do. As you improve your self-worth you can have what's possible: a great relationship with yourself – and with another. To love and to be loved.

Ask yourself, If I treated myself like someone I truly loved, what would I do?

8

PRESS THE PAUSE BUTTON

Activating calm with breathing and meditation

BREATHING PLAYS AN IMPORTANT ROLE WHEN IT COMES TO YOUR physical and emotional state. When you are in a state of stress, your breathing tends to be faster which in turn stimulates anxious thoughts. It's like listening to fast music, it's great to get 'pumped up' for exercise, but not so great if you are already feeling overwhelmed and your body and mind are crying out for some peace.

I have found remembering to use my breath as a way of self-soothing incredibly useful. Your breath is always available, day or night and practicing slowing down the breath offers relief quickly. Introducing a sense of calm and slowing everything right down when you are feeling overwhelmed, shocked or anxious gives a wonderful sense of reassurance and release from anxiety and stress. Giving yourself this opportunity to pause is a beautiful gift to yourself. Once you learn to self-regulate, it means that you take your power back, enabling you to feel better without relying on others which is a form of co-dependency.

By intentionally slowing down your breathing, your body and mind have the chance to reclaim some calm, to soothe you.

Take 5 Pause and Practice

Breathing Practice

Use the following steps to slow down your breathing and notice how your mind and body can relax.

Step 1. Sit comfortably or lie down

Step 2. Take a breath in for 4 seconds

Step 3. Hold the breath for 2 seconds

Step 4. Release the breath for 6 seconds

Step 5. Pause briefly before breathing again

Step 6. Practice, practice, practice.

Tips

When you first have a go at slowing down your breathing it may be challenging. Play around with it and see what works for you. You may find using a 3 in, 1 hold and 4 out breathing cycle easier to begin with. See what works for you, as long as you are slowing down your breathing as much as you can comfortably, and the out-breath is longer than the breath in.

When doing this breathing practice, make sure that you are doing belly breathing rather than chest breathing. You can check this by placing one hand on your belly and one hand on your chest. The hand on your stomach should rise when you breathe in and fall when you breathe out. Be patient with yourself as you practice, you will improve over time.

Practice slow breathing once or twice a day, initially at a time when you can relax and are free from distraction. The aim is then to use this skill when you notice you are having a hard time emotionally to activate a calm state, wherever you are and whatever you are doing.

Meditation

I have practiced meditation for 25 years and it is the foundational practice for all the other modalities I have learnt to grow and develop as a person. Whilst I am by no means an excellent meditator, I don't usually sit in the lotus position for hours, I do reap the benefits of the practice. Meditation has given me access to insights and self-awareness, catching negative and positive thought patterns and beliefs. Meditation often gives me respite from whirling thoughts and sitting leaves me feeling calmer and self-assured.

What your mind pays attention to and how it pays attention is another factor that contributes to your emotional and physical state. Much of the time the thoughts playing in your mind and what you are experiencing just happen. This is often referred to as being on autopilot or being 'mindless.' Mindfulness encourages you to notice that 'mind full of thoughts' and notice their quality- are they positive, negative or neutral? Meditation, the formal practice of mindfulness helps you to recognise that thoughts are not reality. You discover that its more useful to avoid fighting against them and instead allow them to flow.

Catching your thoughts and feelings, being able to take a step back from what you are experiencing and not getting too caught up in them, involves being mindful. Mindfulness means paying attention to the present moment and not judging whatever you notice is happening. Not trying to stop and change whatever you are experiencing. Simply watching.

Mindfulness requires you to be aware of what's around you and how your body feels. Meditation is a practice that reels in your thoughts to calm the mind. Meditation is a wonderful way of echoing the truth that you are enough. It is a practice that relies on what is already inside you.

You are not your thoughts.

Your thoughts, the voice in your head is not who you really are. Thoughts come and go, arise and fall away. There's an awareness behind the thoughts that watch them come and go- this is you.

Knowing this can be such a relief because it shows you that you don't have to take your thoughts so seriously. Meditation is a place where you can experience yourself differently. An opportunity to create some distance between yourself and the thought patterns, beliefs and stories that contribute to your suffering.

Meditation involves noticing when your attention has wandered away from the present moment and gently redirecting your attention back to the here and now. It is not a way of attempting to control your thoughts and feelings or to make them go away. Instead, it is allowing them to be present within you and at the same time choosing to shift your attention back to the present moment.

There's a Zen saying that goes,

"You should sit in meditation for twenty minutes a day. Unless you're too busy, then you should sit for an hour."

Taking time out and pressing the pause button helps you to reset especially on the most chaotic or stress-filled days. The best way to take care of the future is to be in the present moment, now. Sometimes you just need to BE for a while, not fixing, not trying to make anything happen. It's a moment-by-moment choice that becomes a way of being. And over time things change.

When you are distracted, you can easily get caught up in thinking and get lost in streams of thought, even falling into the river. The good news is that your mind will settle if you allow it, just like water will settle if left undisturbed. The constant involvement with thinking is what keeps it unsettled. The more you practice meditation, you are likely to find that it's more often the mind that is causing you to suffer and not reality.

According to Kundalini Yoga there are three aspects of mind- positive, negative and neutral.

The positive mind thinks about positive outcomes, where you expect the best. It is your inner eternal optimist.

The negative mind thinks about the worst-case scenario, the just-in-case. It does this to protect you and is an extension of vulnerability.

The neutral mind thinks of the 'bigger picture', it's calm and open. It allows life and the source of love to speak to you.

It is the neutral mind that is cultivated when you practice mindfulness and meditation regularly.

There are many different meditations you can practice and many resources that go deeply into the benefits of meditation which are beyond the scope of this book. So, to get you started I will share a common meditation practice. Your breath is something that is always with you and typically you are not aware of so it until you focus on it and so is a useful point of focus to begin with.

To recap, the formal practice of mindfulness is meditation, and it is a way you can train yourself to be more aware of where your attention goes and gets caught and to redirect your attention to the present moment using a focus of your choice.

Meditation Steps

1. Start by finding a comfortable position. You can either:

    Sit cross-legged on a cushion, allow your back to be straight, keep your eyes closed or half closed and fold your hands comfortably on your lap.

    If you prefer you can sit in a chair with your feet flat on the floor and your hands resting on your lap.

Or you can lie on the floor, on your back with your legs straight out, a few inches apart and your arms at your sides, preferably with palms facing up.

2. Check in with how you are now, thoughts, emotions, and sensations.

    Ask yourself, what am I experiencing right now? What's my internal weather? What thoughts are around, what feelings and body sensations do you notice? Allow yourself to acknowledge and observe these experiences without judgement and without attempting to change them or make them go away. Practice this for 30 seconds to 1 minute

3. Now spread out your focus to become aware of your breathing.

    Focus on the sensations of your breath as you inhale and exhale. Notice the cool air entering your nostrils as you breathe in, and the warm air being released as you exhale. Notice your belly or ribcage rising and falling. If your mind wanders, notice what thoughts, feelings or sensations it has focussed on without trying to change them or making them go away. Acknowledge their presence by saying "I see you, or I feel you" and now I am going to refocus on my breath. Then let go of your attention and focus back on your breath. Do this for 1 to 2 minutes.

4. Now spreading out your focus from the breath to become aware of the whole body.

    Allowing the body to be just as it is. Spreading out your focus to any activity within the mind and allowing it to be just as it is. Becoming aware now of the space surrounding the body, any sense of warmth or coolness, the sounds around you and the ground beneath you. Opening your eyes gently and noticing the shapes and colours around you. Gradually opening up to your whole experience in this moment.

5. Take a moment to reorient yourself and continue with the activities of your day.

Remember that it is not possible to have a 'blank mind'. Your mind will wander, that's what minds do. The practice of meditation is to gently escort the mind back to the present and the task at hand, for example to focus on the breath or a mantra. To cultivate awareness of where your mind has wandered to and bring it back.

The Art of Receiving

You can't breathe out and not in again.

Take a moment to consider this.

There is a balance to everything upheld by the universal law of equilibrium. In modern-day society however, this law is not widely acknowledged or taught. You are taught about the virtues of giving but not the receiving so it's hard to take things in. Giving more than receiving has become normalised and therefore the damage this does is not easily recognised. It is perpetuated down family lines and then into your relationships.

If you have been in a relationship or situation that was not reciprocal, that was unhealthy and causing it to be out of balance then you are likely to have given much more than you received. You may be used to pouring yourself out and not being filled up. I want you to know that you deserve more, and that it is safe to ask for more. And more than just enough.

Practising the art of receiving gently builds up your receiving muscles. You are on this Earth to thrive, to enjoy life and you cannot do that if you are constantly in deficit. Receiving by noticing how delicious it feels to take a breath in is one way, another is connecting to yourself through meditation.

Here are a few more:

Saying thank you when someone compliments you and fully taking it in.

Allowing people to help you, even if you can do it yourself you don't have to!

Choosing to believe that you deserve all good things.

When I eventually told my good friend Samantha, who had been friends with us both for several years, that my husband had left and the way he did, she was sad. She wasn't just sad about the situation; she was sad that I hadn't confided in her sooner. She felt she had missed an opportunity to support me when I was in turmoil and pain, she didn't like the thought that she could have been there for me if I had let her know.

Even though I knew how much of a good friend she was and how much love she brought to all of us (dogs included), I couldn't face telling her because I felt ashamed. Looking back, I was also in shock and living in a kind of 'trauma bubble' that took me some time to emerge from, even so it was the thoughts around not being good enough that made me resist receiving her kindness.

The wonderful visceral sense of being loved and cared for that I felt as soon as I reached out and received support was deeply nourishing. Through my amazing friends and family, I was able to see that there was no need to be ashamed and that they wanted to help me because of who I am. I was not defective, I was not unworthy, in fact the complete opposite.

Part 3

EXPAND AND FEEL

9

EXPANSION- RECONNECTION TO YOURSELF

"How did you do it?"

"How did you take your power back?" was the very thoughtful question my friend Lesley posed.

The answer gathered in my head like pieces of a jigsaw puzzle coming into view. I knew I had all the pieces and had not yet put them together until that moment of inspired clarity. They shuffled in my mind, found their right places and suddenly, the full picture was formed. It was like completing a game of solitaire on a computer when you realise you've won. You can choose to allow the computer to finish the game. It then feverishly sorts all the remaining cards and puts them on the correct piles and finishes enthusiastically by offering you congratulations with a triumphant 'dadaah'.

I realised that if I had a map of how I did it, how I went from shock, disbelief and despair to understanding, acceptance and peace. That meant I could find the pattern and the connecting pieces for you as well. This realisation filled me with excitement and contentment, the same feeling I get when I see the snowdrops peeking through the ground in my garden in late January early February. Seeing these little shoots heralds the coming of the spring, lighter days, optimism and opportunities for more play after the darkness of winter.

How did I do it- My Map

After the initial shock of separation, I gathered as much information as I could, feeling into what was nurturing for me to listen to and keep and what was unhelpful, in an attempt to understand what was going on and why.

As my husband said that he "*did not have to answer any of my questions*", I didn't have much to go on to accept and make peace with this sudden, unexplained devastation that had ripped through my life like a tornado without warning. I knew I needed to process it and yet didn't know where to start.

At first, I was outwardly focused on what I could do or be differently to repair our relationship. The frustration and hope of making everything OK again consumed me. All I could think about was how to save my marriage and the life I knew. I clung onto it tight, like a baby gripping onto your finger with all its might. I realised later that it was a blessing that he refused to give me any answers because the answers I needed were never going to come from him. It was me that had them all along.

I read book after book trawling the pages for clues on how to repair our relationship. How To Save Your Marriage, 7 Keys to a Happy Marriage, Atlas of the Heart to name just a few and yet as I read them a theme emerged that I was not expecting.

At the same time, my daughter came across a catchy mantra that she shared with me, and it stuck. Whenever I fell into doom and gloom, the words were repeated back to me like an enthusiastic cheerleader; in a playful, repetitive, inspiring ditty kind of tone that lifted me out of my funk.

Rejection is protection

Rejection is protection, rejection is protection, rejection is protection.

Those words comforted me and created curiosity within me as I questioned, 'What am I being protected from?' And as time went on and my attempts to heal the rift in my marriage failed, I knew that I was being protected from going backwards. I understood that not all storms come to disrupt your life, some come to clear your path.

I wasn't expecting to discover that there are ingredients to a happy marriage that I hadn't been experiencing and that you can indeed have your cake and eat it too. When I felt full and satiated from my profound inquiry, I had a good sense as to what hadn't been working in my marriage. I also realised what I need to feel connected, nurtured and loved and that it was OK to want those things.

I went on to listening to my feelings and then deeply exploring my emotions, this is a skill that I have honed over recent years. Like many people, perhaps including yourself, I had always shied away from truly expressing my feelings and therefore my needs for fear of some kind of negative response or consequence.

For example, I was so worried in 2014 about telling my parents that I was quitting my job and going self-employed that I wrote an email outlining my reasons! Even though I was following my joy, it was a daunting prospect to share and carry out.

The difference between feelings and emotions however is that feelings are mental reactions and can be hidden, whereas emotions are physical states that can pop up at any moment as well as being so deep that it can take a lifetime to connect with them and understand them.

Emotions can seem overwhelming and scary, like a black hole that you could get sucked into whilst kicking and screaming and never remerge. I have discovered that the best way to work with emotions is to allow them the space they need to fully flow. When you have experienced and felt the emotion, sat with it without running away, it then has a chance to dissipate. Emotions or e-motions are energy in motion and need to flow. If they stagnate and get stuck, they can become unknown entities that are scary until they are exposed to the clarifying light of day.

To start expressing my emotions, I had to identify what they were and label them. Then feeling those emotions without judgement and accepting that they were there as messengers sent to help me not hinder me.

I discovered exploring my feelings and writing them down layer after layer was very cathartic and healing. Each time I explored my emotions and feelings, the thoughts and beliefs I had attached to them and what stories I was telling myself, the greater understanding and compassion I had for myself.

I decided to write in a journal every day so that I could feel the relief of releasing my thoughts. To begin with all writing happened sat tucked up in bed, my safe cosy space. I got a cup of tea and a glass of water just in case I was there for quite a while, ensured tissues were handy and got out my journal and pen.

I dated the page at the top and poured out my thoughts. Angry thoughts, despairing thoughts, hopeful thoughts. Dating the page helped me to go back and evaluate and assess my progress. To help me recognise changes in my perception towards myself and my experiences.

I gained so many insights by making space to write. For example, it amazed me how you can get so used to and accepting of the behaviours of others, especially when they are not healthy or kind. Often in the midst of life words and deeds go under the radar, only to be flagged when either you decide, or life nudges you to be open to truly listening.

For a long time, I was in denial. I sugar-coated the unpleasant things and often blamed myself instead of facing the truth of the situation. I tried to prove myself worthy in the hope of being recognised. Only when looking back with fresh eyes and a self-loving heart did I distinguish the reality. I appreciate that hindsight is a wonderful thing and so having a record of your thoughts and feelings to look back on from a place of self-compassion can be very healing and liberating.

I wrote in my journal every day, mainly in the morning, as well as when thoughts popped randomly into my head. Some days I was pensive and calm, I took time to consider what I truly thought. I would tap my pen end to end on the journal from which clarity arose, just like the sound and rhythm of a shamanic drum creates the space for new inquiry and insight.

Other days I wrote through gritted teeth frantically and angrily as smoke almost rose from the page. If I knew that I had a lot to release I would then take a separate piece of paper and write a letter, pouring out my thoughts and then I'd burn it. Watching the paper set alight and the fire curling the words on the page with a red glow, reducing it to ash helped me to release them and the pain they described to the Universe. I knew that holding that anguish inside my body was toxic to me and this ritual made space for new, healthier thoughts to arise.

Days where I was a puddle of tears, gulping big breaths and sobbing my heart out were particularly tough and yet were very cleansing. Big realisations and the particularly thoughtless actions of others brought up a sense of being unsafe that turned on the tap. In those moments I would use my tools for self-soothing, to let myself know that I was fundamentally safe and OK. For example, I would put one hand on my heart and one hand on my stomach and repeat this mantra:

I am safe

I am loved

All is well

As I repeated those words over and over and felt the warmth of my hands soothing me, the big gulping gasps for air turned to slow deep breaths and my heart went from galloping to a gentle rhythmic beat. My body unfurled from a tense bent-inward position to a straighter, softer and more confident posture.

From that space, I wrote about what I needed and wanted. I was renewed in my resolve to learn and grow from this experience and not to be bitter or broken by it. My writing had a pattern to it and when I look at my journals now, I can see the trajectory my healing journey took.

It started with themes around questioning what am I going to do? Concerns about everything I had lost or was going to lose- security, love, money, our home.

Then thoughts shifted to how unfair it seemed that my world had been turned upside down and it was not my choice, not my decision.

There was confusion, despairing and grief, missing connection, fear of the future, disappointment, hope and then acceptance.

Writing was a huge comfort to me, and I was able to express a lot. Eventually my writing practice moved from my bed to the dining room table where it has remained. The change from being cocooned in my bedroom to a more communal space in the house signalled a positive shift in healing for me.

One of my biggest challenges in the early months was talking about what had happened, even to those who were closest to me. I was utterly mortified. I was extremely sheepish about reaching out to talk or let people know about the dramatic change in my life. I imagined that people would wonder what was wrong with me. I truly thought that I would be judged as being defective in some way.

Luckily the road rose up to meet me and my amazing Mum, family and wonderful friends rallied around and bolstered me. They acted like scaffolding around a sacred monument, holding me up, protecting me, bringing food, and chocolate and soothing me with their words of kindness and wisdom.

How does that make you feel?

It was during a weekend retreat to Scotland to visit my business mentor Mandy that another guest and business colleague Rachael asked me a profound question. The answer to which was like a key unlocking the door to my future happiness.

I wasn't sure if I could face going to the retreat at first, I was still in shock. The trip had been planned for quite a while and Mandy reassured me. She suggested to treat the time away as a nurturing retreat. I could relax, be creative and be in the company of some great women. No expectations. No cooking. Being taken care of, in a beautiful space, in a gorgeous part of the country.

I went along and I am so glad that I did. True to her word Mandy made my whole stay comfortable and easy-going. She listened to my woes, offered words of wisdom, fed me gorgeous food and gently started my healing process through helping me create a series of empowering multimedia art pieces. Being in her presence and watching her work was inspiring.

One morning after a walk, I was in the dining room with Rachael waiting for everyone else to come in for an activity. We were talking about my situation at home and how for several months leading up to my husband's departure I had felt unsupported and put down by some of his comments about my business plans.

Rachael reflected back to me that I seemed disheartened by this and that I had been putting up with negative energy that was making me feel small and contracted. She then invited me to feel how it would be different to do what I wanted to do, with encouragement and support.

"How does that make you feel?" she said. *"To allow yourself to be fully you?"*

Suddenly, seemingly out of nowhere I felt my whole being lift and rise, upwards and outwards. A lightness, an expansion, like I grew 10 feet taller with a great big Cheshire cat grin on my face. This visceral sensation of body and mind surprised me, it was a wonderful feeling of hope and joy. Yet it scared me. I knew in that moment a choice was on the horizon. A choice I would need to make peace with, so that I could hold that feeling of expansiveness and freedom. I would need to let my husband go.

The promise of that profound uplifting sensation stayed with me. It was like I had walked through the wardrobe in Narnia, into a whole new magical world. I knew that I could return there and eventually I did.

After 3 months, once the shock had settled and I could eat properly again, I found the courage to feel the fear of the unknown and allowed myself to dream about what my new life would look like. I resolved to use this experience as an opportunity to follow what makes my heart sing, to flow through life using my skills and tune into guidance if I got stuck.

I also knew in my bones, at the very core of me that I had an abundance of love to give and share. I knew that I couldn't and didn't want to keep all that love to myself. I decided to employ love and use it in every decision and action I took. To be guided by love.

Once my emotions were more balanced and I had a clearer idea of who I am and what I want, my creativity really began to rise, and I knew that writing a book would be a great way for me to express myself and everything I have learnt. I was back in the driving seat of my life, the ruler of my world again, autonomous and in contented alignment. And with the added attraction of helping others with my humble offering, a book felt like a good way to spread my love into the world.

I also challenged myself to do new things and activities that I would have previously relied on other people to do. Small things built my confidence like collecting parcels from depots that meant I had to navigate my least favourite roundabouts. Picking up my son in the middle of the night from a party when he called for assistance, and a different kind of challenge: Hot Pod Yoga.

I tested myself. Felt the fear and acted.

At times I was surprised at the ways my heartbreak and separation had affected me, how much it had knocked my confidence and caused me to feel vulnerable and uncertain in surprising situations. When my emotions popped up unexpectedly although they initially phased me, I used the tools I have learnt to support me. Over time I was able to cultivate deeper levels of inner strength to ride the waves of fear. One wave at a time.

Imagine a friendly, open-minded and welcoming group of people inviting you into a warm and cosy space to relax. No problem you would think. My system thought otherwise!

Inside the pod was lovely, it was dark except for some pretty string lights and set up with everything I needed. Mats, blocks, blankets. Gentle music was playing, and a lovely aroma wafted from a diffuser. I had my water and fluffy socks and my lovely friend Samantha beside me. The dome shape of the dark purple pod was cocooning and high enough not to be claustrophobic.

And then the facilitator zipped us in, snug as a bug. The sound of the zip closing the pod and shutting off my exit caused a ripple effect in my mind and body. Suddenly the darkness felt scary, the uncertainty of what was going to unfold started my mind racing, the sound of the fans loud in my ears, the heat seemed to rise as high as the Sahara Desert. I felt trapped inside with a large group of strangers with the expectation to release and relax.

I wanted to run away and yet the wiser part of me started to whisper reassurances. Take a sip of water. Close your eyes and breathe. Press your thumb and forefingers together to move the energy. Lay down, feel the support of the Earth holding you.

As I did so, I felt more in control and calmer.

When I sat up and opened my eyes, I leant over to the kind-eyed facilitator and said, "*What if I freak out?*" and with a knowing smile, he gently said "*It's just a zip, if you need to leave you can. For now, how about you have a go at riding the waves of discomfort and using your breath.*"

That extra pep talk soothed my worried inner child and I was then able to watch my thoughts and body have moments of fear and met them with breathing slowly and deeply.

I settled into the class after a while, my shoulders gently melted down from my ears inviting my whole body to follow suit and soften. I noticed the areas where I was holding tension like my jaw and face and let go. My mind stopped racing and became quiet. The sounds in the pod went from a cacophony to focussed as I tuned into the instructions being given.

In the end I felt restored; warm. Loose in my body and my mind free from chatter. I really enjoyed the experience and had a big sense of achievement for having stayed and worked through my initial discomfort.

Looking Through the Nine Star Ki Lens

Everyone journeys through life's challenges according to their unique blend of circumstances, skills and tools, attachment styles, past experiences and archetypal patterns. Your Nine Star Ki archetypes can go a long way to helping you discover and recognise how you are likely to think, feel and respond to stressful situations. If you are out of balance, they show you how to come back into equilibrium so that you can handle these situations with grace.

Reconnecting with my truth, the essence of who I am and how I show up in the world was made easier when I used the Nine Star Ki Guiding Stars or energetic archetypes as a guide. Knowing who I am through this lens helps me to be kinder and less judgemental towards myself.

The archetypes are on a continuum or scale, full of different variations of personalities. Each archetype can be described in its main form and then further defined by its characteristics.

Let's take water as an example.

Water can take many forms and its essential purpose is to support life, without it you would not survive. On one side of the scale water can be large swelling waves that crash down and batter the sand, powerful and ferocious. On the other end of the scale majestic icebergs, cold, hard and travelling down deep into the sea. In between you can find bubbling brooks, snowflakes, waterfalls, calm deep lakes and trickling streams.

Water is most useful though when it is in a still and calm state so that it can be utilised for drinking and bathing in.

Whilst all varieties are welcome, residing in the middle of the continuum offers the best opportunity for feeling balanced and centred; that you have autonomy in your life and are not being held to ransom by your fears or carried away by your ego. If you spend too long at the extremes it can be detrimental and like most things in life, its preferable to aim for the middle ground like Goldilocks and the porridge, not too sweet not to sour, just right!

You will travel along the continuum at different points in your life, even fleeting moments in your day. Being aware of what state you are in and how to get back into equilibrium is a skill and requires practice. Once you are aware of what to look for you are halfway there- awareness is key.

Once I understood the full scope of who I am, at my core, in my natural, healthy and balanced state, I recognised what was guiding me. It is me. It is you. It has been this way the whole time. It's the version of you that is connected to the Universal life-giving, life-affirming force of Love. The version that is open to being authentic and whole.

Reconnecting to your wholeness

When you experience a significant change in your life, like a breakup or ending of a friendship it comes with a sense of loss. That there is a piece that is missing. This can arise from a tendency to put people on pedestals in your mind. Because you perceive them to have more of a particular quality than you have, when they are no longer a big part of your life you feel the absence of it.

I always perceived my ex-husband as adventurous; he would go surfing, climbing, and drive to far-flung places just to explore. When we were no longer going on these adventures with him, I worried that life would become boring.

What I did not give myself credit for was that I am adventurous in different ways. I showed my adventurous side when I took a risk and became self-employed. I am adventurous with my ideas, new ways of thinking and bucking the trend like organising a baby naming ceremony instead of a traditional christening for our daughter long before they were popular.

When someone or something is not connected to you anymore, it does not mean that you personally have broken apart or are no longer whole. You were and are always whole. It is your self-awareness and self-worth that may need to be repaired so that you can reconnect with all the forgotten or disowned parts of you.

Recognising Wholeness Exercise

Write down a trait that you admire in someone.

It could be being kind, having a sense of humour, playful, assertive, great communicator.

Underneath this trait, write down all the ways that you display this quality. Recognising that there are many variations to each one.

Where can you take full ownership of the quality?

Notice now how differently you feel about yourself.

Write down what you now recognise about yourself that's different to before.

10

EMOTIONS

Feelings Matter, You Matter

HOW YOU FEEL IS IMPORTANT. ALLOWING YOUR FEELINGS TO BE A guide enables you to align with the truth of who you are. The 'You-ness' of You, your inner being. Your feelings show you *who* you are allowing yourself to be right now because of the thoughts you are thinking. Your feelings help you to discern if your thoughts match up with your intentional way of being.

For me, my intentional way of being is to be guided by love and so whenever I have thoughts that are less than loving I reach for a kinder, more compassionate or loving perspective. Whilst all emotions are absolutely valid and should be felt, it is also beneficial for your well-being and potential to come back into alignment with your truth.

Emotions are energy in motion or e-motion and need to be able to flow freely and be expressed for you to stay in a healthy balance. Being in balance and grounded means that you are not so easily swayed or knocked by uncomfortable or triggering events, and you can bounce back or come back to your centre, the core of you, more quickly and easily should you lose your balance.

In nature willow trees are a good example of this. On windy days they can be bashed by the wind and rain causing them to bend and sway and yet if their roots are strong, they come back to standing again.

Emotions are reactions linked to your fight, flight and freeze response and are largely unconscious until something happens to trigger them. All emotions tell you something about yourself and your situation and so as such are valuable guides. Triggering events can be small or more significant. The term 'triggered' refers to having an emotional reaction to an event that reminds you of something that previously made you feel unsafe.

Your emotions start as sensations in the body whereas your feelings are generated from your thoughts about those emotions. Being aware of your emotions, feelings and core needs help you to feel calm, peaceful and happy. Emotions act as a guide for you. They alert you to your inner landscape. They invite you to explore what is going on deep inside you. To connect inwards and observe the state of your 'inner weather' as well as your physical landscape.

Being aware and mindful for example, when stress is creeping up on you, that you are holding onto an irritation or conversely that you are all well with the world is important information. Checking in on your feelings is not something widely taught and yet it is so beneficial to maintaining your vitality.

Knowledge is power. Awareness is key.

Once you are aware of and understand what is going on within you and what steps you can take to improve it, you have sovereignty over yourself. You have taken back the wheel and are in the driving seat of your life. Being aware of your underlying emotions enables you to make the next link between what you truly need and want. To understand what your non-negotiables are in life so that you can conquer and then maintain what is important to you.

Take 5 Pause and Practice

Inner Landscape Check-In

I invite you to take an inner landscape inventory, to survey the land of your body and mind.

Stop any activity that you are doing. Put down your pen, phone or laptop. Sit or stand comfortably and close your eyes.

What do you immediately notice?

How does your body feel? Are there any obvious tensions?

What thoughts can you catch yourself thinking? Are they positive, worried, self-deprecating?

Does pausing give you relief?

Take a few deep breaths now.

How does that alter your inner landscape?

Breathing or breath is the bridge between body and mind. It helps you to connect the two. It assists you in regulating your nervous system from parasympathetic to sympathetic. From stressed and on high alert for threats to calm, peaceful and safe.

When your nerves feel jangled, your stomach is in knots and your mind is like spaghetti the easiest and most effective way to bring some comfort and soothing is to simply be and breathe.

Checking in regularly throughout the day is a wonderful way of tracking your progress from catastrophic to calm, from tense to tender and panic to peace.

The Three Emotional Systems

Understanding how you can manage and balance your emotions helps to turn your focus towards cultivating self-compassion and self-love. This is because when you know which emotional system you are currently using, you can choose to step out of it or stay with it. Being aware of your emotional state enables you to consider whether what you are thinking or doing serves you or how it is not serving you.

How do you know if your emotions are out of balance and need regulating? Professor Paul Gilbert answered this question by developing the Three Emotional Systems model, using neuroscience research, receiving a Knighthood for this valuable and insightful work.

The model describes how your evolved brain has three emotional systems that you switch between and that each one is associated with different regions of the brain and different chemistry.

The Three Emotional Systems are:

- A threat and self-protection system
- A drive and resource-seeking system
- A soothing and contentment system

The threat system is always on the lookout for threats to your safety and that of your loved ones. It aims to protect you by preparing you to run away from physical danger. It is also activated by non-physical threats such as worrying or not being able to do things. It is connected to feelings of anger, fear, anxiety and disgust. Your body produces adrenaline when you are in this system.

If your threat system dominates the others, you can often feel 'under threat', 'on guard' or constantly anxious. When you are in threat mode your thinking becomes very narrow and negative and your mind becomes unable to move out of its negative narrow focus. It is difficult to think rationally in threat mode because this type of thinking involves sophisticated processing and time. In threat mode your thinking is quick and reactive. That's why it's important to be gentle with yourself when you are experiencing distressing emotions, your mind was not designed to think rationally when under stress or in danger.

The drive system is focused on getting the resources needed for you to survive and thrive. It aims to motivate you and spur you on to try new things, to achieve goals and is reward-based: you feel good afterwards, like experiencing those joyful 'high five' moments. It is connected to feelings of excitement, focus and wanting.

Your body produces dopamine when you are in this system the effect of which can be mimicked by stimulants such as caffeine.

If you spend most of your time in drive, it can send you into overdrive, the compulsion to do more and do better and you can get trapped in "I must achieve, I must do better, I must do, do, do". Then when something stops you from achieving you can become distressed and self-critical – this can then push you into threat mode.

The soothe system, helps you to manage stress and bond with others. It has a calming influence on both the threat and the drive systems, helping to quieten them down when they are overactive. It relates to feelings of contentment, safety and connection to others. You can tell when you are in the soothe system when you are chilled out, feeling safe, calm and content.

Your body produces opiates and oxytocin- the feel-good chemical in this state. The soothe system can only operate when there are no threats to your safety and when you have sufficient resources for the time being. When this system is activated, you can soothe yourself in times of difficulty and suffering. To feel safe including feeling able to reach out for support from friends, family and sources of help.

Experiences of kindness, care and compassion stimulate this system. Investing in yourself by spending time on activities that make you feel content, safe and cared for brings your soothe system online balancing your emotions and improving your well-being.

Take 5 Pause and Journal

Draw 3 circles on a blank piece of paper or in your journal and name them threat, drive and soothe. Write in the appropriate circle the brief answers to the following questions. You can then expand your thinking further by journalling on each question.

What triggers your own systems of threat, drive and soothe?

How much time do you spend in each of these systems?

What can you introduce to work towards a better balance between the systems?

How the model gave me clarity

I noticed this model explained the stages that I went through during my breakup. The emotional systems can be used to give you an insight into where you are emotionally and what system you are operating from when you are upset.

When my husband left, it felt like a huge threat to my safety and to the safety of my family. I was worried about maintaining a home, and where the money would come from to pay the bills. I was anxious about my children's well-being and emotional states. I was angry at being put in the situation I faced.

My confidence took a huge knock and I felt extremely vulnerable. Things that seemed so easy before were quite terrifying now. There was also a level of shame and anxiety about what other people would think of me and the situation. I felt threatened by embarrassment. At first when people asked where he was, I said he was away for work, not wanting to deal with or face the questions that I didn't even know the answers to.

Then the drive system kicked in. My wonderful family and friends encouraged me to stop thinking about him and start thinking about me. To put down focusing on how to repair my relationship and to get my ship in order. To consider the resources that I needed and to decide on a plan of action. They reminded me that I needed some solid ground underneath my feet before I could move forward with anything else. That looking after myself and my children's welfare were my priorities.

The drive system gave me the fuel I needed to face some very uncomfortable and to me, mortifying activities such as seeking government help. I had many difficult yet important conversations that took up hours and hours. I spoke to my mortgage company, creditors, the bank, utility companies, and local council services just to name a few.

I sobbed on the phone to the Citizens Advice Bureau who were absolutely amazing. They managed to manoeuvre my ship off the rocks and into safer waters. They offered help and support in a myriad of different ways. I was so touched by their kindness and extremely thankful for all the services available to me.

The drive system propelled me to look for a suitable job so that I could be available for the kids, whilst at the same time keeping a roof over our heads and food on the table. My emotional state included determination, bravery and grit which helped me to work through the toughest days and get into a position where I was out of survival and on my way to thriving.

Once my system recognised that the kids and I were safe and had the resources, tools and support in good order, then I was able to rebuild. I could access more readily the soothe emotional system and I could begin to see how I could be content again.

I was soothed by the simple things like having plenty of toilet roll, fat balls in the bird feeder and petrol in my car. These became my measuring sticks of contentment, of doing OK. Then my measuring sticks transitioned to feeling more settled in my job, Iris managing more

119

days at college and Alfie passing his driving test. Eventually, this led to me feeling content watching TV alone at night, talking openly to friends and confidently planning out future activities.

I, like you always had access to my soothing system, however it took much more effort to be mindful to go there during the days of heightened stress. An effort definitely worth making.

11

YOUR CORE NEEDS

Looking Through the Nine Star Ki Lens

How do you know then, which emotions to look out for? The ones that tend to pop up most and cause you pain and suffering? I will introduce you to a few ways that can assist you with this including utilising your Nine Star Ki inner or heart number.

Let's begin by looking at each of the 5 elements- water, earth, wood, metal and fire. I will share which emotions are a sign of imbalance and each of the elements' associated core needs and drivers.

Your inner or heart number is the energy of your inner landscape, the seat of your emotions and can give you lots of information about how to self-regulate and self-soothe and what to look for as indicators of being stressed and out of balance.

You can think of the emotional driver as similar to Gilbert's drive system.

Refer to your Nine Star Ki numbers as illustrated in the chart on page 16 and look at what element your inner or heart number is. For example, 1 is Water, 2,5,8, are Earth, 3,4 are Wood/ Tree, 6,7 are Metal and 9 is Fire.

Elements- Core Needs

Core needs are the feelings and tasks that each element thrives on, incorporating them into your life as much as possible enables you to feel aligned, purposeful and content.

- **Fire** needs to feel joy, to feel close to others and to receive warmth and love
- **Water** needs to be able to assess risk, feel fear and then respond appropriately
- **Earth** needs to nourish others and be nourished, cared about and supported
- **Wood** needs to learn and grow; to be assertive and have good boundaries
- **Metal** needs to be able to process loss and grief and take the rich lessons from them to feel whole. Also needs acknowledgement and recognition for their achievements.

When you know what you fundamentally need to be in a balanced state of body, mind and spirit then you can work towards cultivating more of that energy in your life. When you know what to look for, you are able to recognise it when it appears. You can confidently ask for your specific needs to be met because you know it benefits your well-being.

Being aware of how you feel and what your natural state is when in balance is very useful, you can use the emotions and thoughts you experience as a guide, like a litmus test. When you then find yourself out of balance it is easier to spot and remedy.

Prolonged periods of stress are detrimental to your health and so whilst it is normal to have times of stress and imbalance it is best not to stay stuck there. Being out of balance can cause confusion and anxiety, conflicts in your relationships, and a lack of drive and purpose, perhaps leading to issues at work and physical symptoms such as headaches and stomach issues.

Emotions of Elements out of balance

Fire- Lack of joy/Sadness

.**Water**- Fear/Abandonment

Earth- Sympathy/Worry

Wood- Anger/Frustration

Metal- Grief/Loss

Signs of imbalance can start off subtly and then get louder and more intense until you address them. Your thoughts and experiences are a good measure of whether you are moving out of balance.

Each element has clues to imbalance and so if you start to experience these warning signs or questions coming to mind it's time to pause and take stock.

Here are the challenging aspects of each stage and some of the remedies to help rebalance them.

Water- fear, lack of trust and loneliness. **Remedy** is to do nothing, float, relax.

Wood- anger, feeling blocked and misunderstandings. **Remedy** is to define your goals and act.

Fire- lack of joy, heartbreak and feeling rejected. **Remedy** is to explore what makes your heart sing.

Earth- worry, weak boundaries and lack of support. **Remedy** is to look at what needs to be organised or completed.

Metal- anxiety, grief and lack of self-esteem. **Remedy** is breathwork, letting go and predictability.

Let's get more specific and look at what nourishes and regulates each of the 9 archetypes' emotions

Nine Star Ki Inner Numbers are Nourished by:

1 **Water**- is nourished by silence, being and allowing time for thinking and feeling deeply and a sense of freedom beyond fear.

2 **Earth**- a sense of connection, gathering friends and family together, sharing food and catching up with each other.

3 **Tree**- need support to be independent, mutually exclusive qualities that are needed for growth and for you to thrive, require adventure.

4 **Tree**- talking and sound, writing and other creative and artistic ways of expression.

5 **Earth**- receiving positive attention such as encouragement or being acknowledged. This helps you to shine.

6 **Metal**- a core values system to follow, minimalist- clear and tidy space, quality- both in terms of items and time, truthfulness.

7 **Metal**- seeks harmony and needs to reflect on what they do and don't like, to exercise and experience touch like massage or hugs.

8 **Earth**- love books, libraries and mysteries, research and history. Looking back to bring things into the present- daydreaming, contemplating, health and the human body.

9 **Fire**- being centre stage, having a range of fun activities to do and spreading love through being a good friend or making people laugh.

It's reassuring to be mindful of how your emotional needs dance with each other, as when they pop up you can recognise them and will not be so easily fazed by them.

For example, Iris, whose Nine Star Ki is 4.3.6 had a discombobulating experience with her college tutor, whom she admired and felt comfortable with normally. This day her tutor had a lot on her mind and was not her usual self. Iris picked up on her tutor's change in energy as she is sensitive and empathic, it felt disconcerting and confusing to her. Iris took it to heart and didn't feel like she could talk to her tutor as freely as usual.

Feeling unable to express her thoughts and therefore missing out on receiving reassurance and recognition, did not meet Iris's emotional needs and so she felt somewhat bereft. It subtly reminded her of the feelings of grief she had around her dad leaving the family home and not receiving the answers and reassurance that she needed from him.

When Iris realised that she was taking on her tutors' energy unnecessarily and was inadvertently allowing it to trigger her, she could release that burden and she felt a lot better. She remembered a saying 'Not your monkeys, not your circus', and it made her laugh, which in turn shifted her emotions back to a more positive, balanced state.

Emotional Intelligence

In 1995 Daniel Goleman published the groundbreaking book, Emotional Intelligence and shone a spotlight on the importance and power of emotions. Through his research he was able to show that your success in life is based as much if not more on your ability to manage your emotions than your intellectual capabilities. He defines Emotional Intelligence as consisting of five skills: knowing your emotions, managing emotions, motivating yourself, recognising emotions in others and handling relationships.

From his work a new field of psychology was born called Positive Psychology where it was discovered that positive emotional states broaden your thinking. Negative emotions on the other hand can prevent you from reaching the states you need to access problem-solving and creativity.

Generating feelings of appreciation, love, care and compassion, enables you to experience a deeper level of intuition and insight for more effective decisions in day-to-day life. Positive emotions like love, appreciation, care and compassion help to balance your nervous system.

Without experiencing the wisdom of listening to your heart and enhancing your emotional intelligence, your mind is more susceptible to reactive emotions such as anger, fear, insecurity and blame.

You can learn to recognise emotions and attitudes that drain you and replace them with more positive ones that provide enlightened perspectives.

The mind rationalises- it can make you feel that you are justified in being angry.

The heart is softer- it whispers to you to you with quiet common sense.

It takes courage to listen to your heart.

The key is to use emotion in a balanced way. To listen to what your feeling is telling you and then work out how to act upon it in a way that is beneficial for the situation, your life and the world around you.

It may be though that even before you learn to recognise your emotions, a reminder is in order; A reminder for you to truly know that it is worth the effort, that you are awesome. That you are more than brilliant, that you are loved unconditionally simply for being you and exactly as you are. I potentially need to remind you that your light may currently be dimmed, that does not mean it has been lost. It is there, hidden under layers of fears, doubts, blame, shame and untrue stories that you have believed for so long.

Sometimes there is a necessity to let life crack you open to reveal your power and beauty within.

The Reason for Mistrust in Yourself

The Negative Bias and Your "Tinker Brain"

Your human brain is amazing, and its primary job is to keep you alive. The aim of keeping you safe and out of danger is paramount. Whilst humans have evolved and developed the capacity to think about things, to ruminate, worry and consider, the brain has not evolved to maintain a healthy or positive mindset. Instead, you have a "threat mindset" that is hard-wired, otherwise known as the negativity bias which fixes and focuses on what can go wrong.

Rick Hanson, PhD describes the negativity bias as, *"We're Velcro for difficult experiences and Teflon for pleasant ones."*

This means that you often receive messages that say, *"What can go wrong?"*. Your brain defaults to looking for negativity so that you remain cautious and therefore 'safe'. Then, unfortunately, in times of stress if left unchecked, the message *"What can go wrong"* turns into *"What's wrong with me?"* and it becomes personalised. If you do not have a solid base of self-love, this negative bias can feed mistrust, thoughts and beliefs. It can be easy to forget how wonderful you are and cover the truth of who you are in thoughts and feelings around unworthiness.

I like to compassionately and playfully call this part of my brain "tinker". A tinker to me is up to mischief and is not being malicious. Catching your negative thoughts in this way and remembering "Oh that's my tinker brain" can diffuse a negative thought thread quickly and painlessly. Instead of being judgemental or resisting your brain's natural ways, you can be kind.

Your tinker brain can be very subtle and get your mind tangled like spaghetti very easily. The trick is to catch yourself in the 'act.' If you don't catch yourself in the moment, it is still useful to catch yourself as soon as you can to bring yourself back to feeling good or neutral again.

Here's a little example for you.

I was driving over to my mums for dinner and needed some petrol. I stopped at the nearest petrol station, pulled up to the pump shut the door and locked the car. I then attempted to open the petrol cap and it was jammed shut. My first thought was it was air-locked and maybe needed a bit of extra strength, so I asked the gentleman in the car in front for some assistance. He pulled it, jiggled it and gave it a shake to no avail. He suggested getting some help from a garage the following morning and to now go and enjoy my dinner.

My petrol light was flashing, and he assured me I'd have enough petrol saying it's amazing how many miles I would get out of it. I left the petrol station and thoughts started whirring away.

"I don't have RAC anymore, perhaps if I call them and re-join, they can come and sort it at mums? But I don't really want that extra cover or expense now. And maybe it wouldn't be covered straight away…"

More thoughts consumed my mind and I felt worried.

"It's Sunday tomorrow and garages will be shut, what if I need something from the shop, what if…."

I got to mum's house and explained my problem. She considered it for a moment and then asked, "So you locked the car?" and went on "Do you usually lock it before getting petrol? Did you try and unlock the car and then open the petrol cap?"

I laughed and said, "Oh if it's that simple, then great!" I went back to my car, unlocked it and low and behold the petrol cap opened with ease.

When I locked the car, as a safety feature it stopped me from opening the petrol cap to put fuel in it. Just like your brain's safety feature is to lock out the positives and focus on the negatives, my car was keeping me safe. Safe from losing petrol. Once I recognised this, I was immediately able to 'fill my tank' back up for many more journeys.

One of my favourite stories to illustrate how your light and your gifts can be hidden is the Golden Buddha.

The Golden Buddha

Many years ago, in Thailand was a temple with a huge Golden Buddha. One day the villagers got word that the Burmese army was about to invade, so they helped the monks cover the Golden Buddha, made of solid gold and very valuable with clay so it looked plain, and the invading army would perceive no value in it.

The army moved through the village and temple and passed by the earthen Buddha and had no reason to steal it. For many years, the army occupied the village with this temple and Buddha. With time there was no longer anyone who remembered that the Buddha was golden.

Then one day in 1957, a young monk was meditating at the base of the Buddha, and a glint of something shining from a small crack in the Buddha caught his eye. The monk excitedly told the other monks, and they used a hammer and chisel to chip away at the clay covering until he revealed the statue was a Golden Buddha.

Over the course of your life, your Golden Buddha, which is a metaphor here for your purpose and light, gets covered in layer upon layer of clay. The heaviest layers are your own limiting self-beliefs that prevent you from following your dreams, living life in alignment with your true self and fulfilling your potential.

The other layers of clay are added by external conditioning from parents and caregivers, schools and teachers, bosses and co-workers, society and the media. Eventually you are so laden with clay that you forget that the Golden Buddha is always there within you.

The secret to finding your Golden Buddha, your higher purpose or golden nature lies in your deepest wounds and cracks. Something occurs in your life such as a loss, major change or tragedy that breaks you open, enough to see the gold within. And so, you start chipping away at the clay to rediscover your true self, to unveil more of the golden you, where your peace and contentment reside.

You can then reconnect with what makes your heart sing, what you value most and what motivates you to get out of bed with a smile on your face. Your curiosity rises along with the excitement about the new opportunities ahead of you, enabling you to discover things that propel you towards your new life and goals. The more you chip away the old unhealthy habits and limiting beliefs, the more gold you will find.

The Power of Emotions

When you have sovereignty over your emotions, you can harness your own power, to stand strong and grounded in your values and convictions. To have the ability to stick up for yourself when needed even if it's scary.

There seems to be a tipping point between staying small and quiet and feeling the fear and doing it anyway. You may not realise you have reached this point until something happens and you approach it in a new way.

I was proud of myself in the moments I became aware that my heart wasn't beating as hard, that I felt calmer and less fuzzy-headed. When I opened an email or had to deal with a challenging conversation, and I felt in control rather than wanting to escape or hide. When I realised that I was doing too much for other people and started to say no and handing the reigns of responsibility back to them.

I had 'tipped over' into an inner sense of strength and determination. Not necessarily a loud roar, more like a rising sense of assurity and contentment.

How you approach this is very much influenced by your personal energy pattern.

For example, having a 1 Water heart number will influence your emotions and the way you respond to situations in specific ways. The way your 1 Water energy dances with your birth and soul numbers will then nuance this.

Being aware of your unique pattern and becoming familiar with it through observing how you approach situations, will help you to access a balanced approach. To respond rather than react.

Remember that reacting means that you have effectively lost your inner balance. Which tends to lead to impulsive outbursts, ill-thought-out actions and feelings of shame or guilt once you have regained your composure. This in turn can erode your self-confidence and feed self-doubt.

When you have a strong reaction to something that in reality is small, benign or not appropriate to the level of your reaction, it is likely to stem from an echo of the past. Noticing for example that you are experiencing a strong emotion to someone leaving a cup in the sink or using the last bit of toilet roll and not replacing it, could be a step towards healing. It alerts you to a deeper hurt underneath.

Once you have identified you are experiencing suffering, for example, that you feel hurt, angry, used, invisible, then you can self-inquire as to the root of that feeling. The antidote to being overwhelmed with strong emotional reactions is to practice identifying your feelings as they happen, until you notice that a 'tipping point' has occurred. Something that tips you over into negative feelings like frustration. Once you get the hang of noticing your emotions and feelings as they are happening, then it's a case of maintenance, which is a lifelong endeavour.

Let's take John as a case study, his Nine Star Ki is 5.1.9

John as a child often felt like an outsider, alone and overlooked. His way of coping with this was to bottle up his deeply held emotions and to withdraw. He came to believe that he was defective due to the way he was treated.

Over time, he began to realise that he was not defective and in fact he had been mistreated. He studied psychology at university and gained a degree which helped him to understand why people behave in the ways they do. The veil of illusion slipped more and more until he began to realise that he was OK, and he did not have to tolerate the abuse. This realisation allowed his emotions to surface.

John's soul number is 9 Fire, a passionate warm and loving energy. His Soul was so fired up one day about the injustice around a conversation he had with a family member that it began to heat up and 'boil' his inner 1 Water- his inner emotions.

Imagine if you will, John's inner emotions as a pan of water over a flame. Eventually the water will boil and cause the lid to come off the pan, producing a lot of steam. The conversation made John so angry that he felt his mounting anger could lead to a heart attack. He was shocked by the force of his emotions boiling over, this came as a wake-up call.

John then began to practice feeling his emotions rising and before they got to boiling point to release the pent-up energy in a more controlled manner. He did this in a variety of ways including using exercise, space clearing and journalling.

My Emotional Journey

My Nine Star Ki is 4.1.8 and although I, like John have 1 Water as an inner/heart number, I experience and heal my emotional responses in ways that are unique to me. My birth and soul numbers also distinguish how I perceive and work through challenging situations.

I grew up with an authoritarian, practical-minded mother and an easy-going father. Being a quiet and gentle person, I was easily influenced by my more dominant mother and I became a typical 'good girl'. As my father modelled 'keeping the peace' I learnt to be compliant and not to express my needs or stand up for myself.

I would experience a visceral fear within when I wanted to do something outside of what I thought was expected of me. This deep fear would often stop me in my tracks and prevent me from going ahead due to being 'frozen' in fear.

On the other side of fear is love. The more that I learnt to love and accept myself the more I was able to confidently move forward with my vision and plans. I am supported by my strong and nurturing 8 Earth energy. A symbol for 8 Earth is the Mountain and inside this mountain is a cave. This cave is where I can go to access my soul's wisdom. I can also imagine standing tall and firm like a majestic mountain.

The tipping point for me was my separation and the mix of feelings that were brought up because of it. Until then I had allowed my emotions to be let out in measured and careful ways, often in a trickle. After my break-up I learnt to allow my emotions to flow. Then as I gained in confidence, I was able to articulate and express them clearly.

John and I's 1 Water heart energy causes us to experience deep feelings, like a well that you can't see the bottom of. We both experienced the fear of the unknown like peering into deep dark water and not wanting to jump in. Yet we both summoned the strength of 1 Water, which is courage, to work through our fears and utilise their wisdom.

Healing the wounds of your childhood or inner child can bring such freedom and empowerment. A happy contented inner child, just like any child tends to be more creative, have more fun and have the freedom to explore their own interests and ideas.

Being aware of your wounds and how they manifest in your daily life, I have found to be immensely useful, and I hope seeing your inner child through the lens of Nine Star Ki will help you too.

Identifying Your Feelings

Emotional Awareness

Emotional awareness involves being conscious of what you are feeling and the ability to observe your responses and behaviours. To understand the emotions involved in any given situation without them taking over you. To connect with your body and listen to its messages. It's about being able to ask yourself 'How am I feeling and why? Why did I say that? What prompted them to say that?'

Checking In on Your Feelings

Being aware of your body's cues, its default reaction when something causes an emotional disturbance within you is extremely useful and very powerful. Having the ability to identify when you are going into a default reaction can help you to skilfully navigate difficult feelings and interactions.

It takes intention, mindfulness and practice to catch yourself in the moment and have the tools to be proactive and respond instead of reacting.

Victor Frankl, an Austrian psychotherapist was a master at this. He wrote the autobiographical, Mans Search for Meaning, after surviving the horrors of the holocaust in Nazis concentration camps. He coined the phrase:

"Between stimulus and response there is a space. In that space is our power to choose our response. In our response lies our growth and our freedom."

There are several things that you need to be aware of to fully appreciate the skill involved in the seemingly simple task that Victor Frankl refers to.

Firstly, you need to allow yourself the space. To give yourself full permission to come out of the shadows and stand in your truth and power. You may be very used to making yourself small, shrinking and not taking up much space. Allowing worrying or negative thoughts to fill your mind preventing the space for new and empowering thoughts to emerge. Feeling comfortable being invisible and expressing few needs. Perhaps you have told yourself that you are content helping other people feel happy. That their happiness is enough for you.

Now however hiding, not getting your needs met and having your feelings discounted is growing thin. You may be beginning to feel ignored, stepped on and even taken advantage of.

Once this feeling of impending, empowering change starts rising within you, it will not be contained. Once you accept that you deserve more, the cat is out of the bag and will not go back in. Rightly so.

Once you recognise that there is a space you can move into and take up, the second step is to recognise your default reactions. A reaction is different to a response.

A reaction happens quickly, often without thought or awareness and can cause you to be impulsive; to say and do things you may later regret or feel guilty about. A response is measured, thought out and felt through and is intentional.

Take 5 Pause and Practice

Checking In on Your Feelings Exercise

When something bothers you, what happens in your body and mind?

Perhaps someone says something or behaves in a way that causes you discomfort. Can you take a moment to explore what goes on inside your body? What sensations do you notice?

Take some deep relaxing breaths, settle into a comfortable and upright posture and bring to mind an interaction or conversation that is causing or has caused you anxiety, anger or anguish.

Scan your body from the tips of your toes to the top of your head and allow yourself to feel the sensations arising. Where do you notice the change in your body?

Is there tightness in your chest?

Do you feel sick?

Heat rising to your cheeks?

A lump in your throat?

Being aware of what happens in your body when under stress, enables you to practice catching yourself as it happens. This takes a little time and effort and is worth it. Having the cues before you react is very helpful in avoiding uttering words or taking actions that you may later regret when you are back in equilibrium.

You are a work in progress, as are all of us and so it's important to remember to be kind to yourself. You are a human being and as so will make mistakes and say and do things that in hindsight you would have done differently. The trick is to have some compassion for yourself and know that you can always begin again. Every moment is a new moment to be embraced.

12

COMPASSION

COMPASSION IS ONE OF THE HIGHEST FORMS OF HUMAN EMOTION. IT is what connects you to others. Compassion embodies a tangible expression of love, like a big warm hug. The feeling of being safe in moments of distress or the experience of profound relief that follows experiencing a deep level of caring. Compassion involves a desire to alleviate suffering and is one of the most valuable skills within emotional regulation you can learn for yourself.

The meaning of compassion is to recognise the suffering of others and then take action to help. There are two types of compassion: the compassion you have for others and the compassion you have for yourself which is self-compassion.

As a society compassion is often shown for others and yet it isn't widely encouraged to be compassionate towards yourself, leaving many people starved of emotional connection and support. Self-compassion is vital in times of stress and suffering. It is also the best defence against one-sided, toxic and unhealthy relationships. When you have self-compassion, gaslighting, negative behaviour and being demeaned will not be tolerated. It's like kryptonite for negative energy.

The Power of Self-Compassion

So why is it so powerful?

Building self-compassion evolves resilience, it strengthens your resolve. It enables you to cultivate an inner strength that is warm, kind and considerate. You begin to care more about yourself and your boundaries. Instead of thinking about the welfare of other people first, you can consider yourself. This is not selfish; it is self-preservation which is your absolute right.

Self-compassion is a superpower, and it is within your power to learn it. Practice using this skill to create a happier, calmer and contented mind. Self-compassion is not simple, if it was then knowing what it is would be enough.

Self-compassion is being able to recognise when you are suffering and accept it. Once you have accepted it then you can use practices and tools to alleviate your suffering. As the saying goes pain is inevitable, suffering is optional.

You can acknowledge you are suffering and that you have the power to do something about it by saying out loud or in your mind the self-compassion mantra.

Self-Compassion Mantra

This is hard and I'm OK.

I've got this.

This mantra helps to ground you in the present moment. It helps you to recognise that you are anxious, worried or distressed and suffering. Once you have conscious awareness then you can take action steps.

Remember your "tinker brain"? It's useful to remind yourself of how it works when you get caught up in self-criticism, doubt or shame. It is not your fault that you think this way. There is a part of your brain called the amygdala that works to protect you and is resistant to change. Whenever you attempt to change a habit or thinking pattern that involves a new goal or direction, the change will automatically be resisted. Knowing this can help you to strengthen your resolve and persevere with being kind to yourself.

Building self-compassion is like building a muscle, you need to give it regular exercise to become stronger. If you don't use the muscle, it will weaken and not work as well.

Mindfulness and meditation are the foundational practices to build self-compassion. They help you to practice slowing down and catching yourself in moments of suffering. This enables you to stand back and observe your thoughts and feelings. Then intentionally redirect or refocus your attention onto more self-compassionate thoughts and ideas. I would wholeheartedly recommend practising mindfulness daily, 5 minutes a day can elevate your well-being.

Take 5 Pause and Journal

When genuinely feeling compassionate you naturally display a soft attentive half-smile, a calm, shoulders-back, head-up stance whilst offering a caring touch and a warm gentle tone of voice.

I invite you to deliberately adopt a compassionate facial expression, body posture and tone of voice and whilst in this compassionate state, journal on the following sentence stems:

- Being self-compassionate towards myself looks like...
- The advice I would give to a friend I deeply care about who was thinking and feeling this way is...
- The compassionate part of me would say..........to the self-critical part

These journal prompts give a voice to the compassionate side of you. A voice that you may not have heard for a long time, bringing new balanced perspectives about the true importance of a situation.

Compassionate Connection

> Connection is "*the energy that exists between people when they feel seen, heard, valued; when they can give and receive without judgement; and when they derive sustenance and strength from the relationship.*"
>
> -Brene Brown

Sharing something very personal with another and revealing what you have been through, sets off a chemical reaction in their mind and body, which creates a connection. It may be quite alien to you to reach out for help when you are upset, especially if you have been discouraged to do so in the past.

Reassuringly, reaching out to trusted friends and family members benefits you both. Instead of feeling like you are bothering someone or are burdensome, which is not true I hasten to add, that you get the support you need to lift a weight off your shoulders. The other person has the gift of being of service and help which feels good. Plus, you build stronger connections and relationships by learning more about each other.

Take 5 Pause and Action

Compassionate Truth Game

Find a partner and a pack of playing cards

The aim of this game is to gently build your confidence around speaking your truth. To say what's on your mind in a safe, encouraging and reciprocal way. It has 3 levels that get progressively more challenging.

Each level is indicated by the number of cards put down, so your partner is aware of what level of sharing you have decided upon. Whilst there is no expectation to go up to a level 3 until you feel comfortable enough to do so, it is worthwhile to attempt it.

The benefit of the game is to show you that sharing your innermost thoughts can bring you relief, and build confidence, self-esteem and connection.

How to Play

Decide on who will go first and then you will each take turns to share.

Consider scenarios, worries or concerns that you would like to bring out into the open. Perhaps a decision you are mulling over or something you have been keeping hidden due to fear of embarrassment or shame.

Decide the level of vulnerability it takes to share this and place the appropriate number of cards in front of your partner.

There are 3 levels to this exercise; easy, medium, hard or sheepish, embarrassed and fearful.

1 card represents something that you feel slightly nervous sharing

2 cards represent something that you feel sheepish saying out loud

3 cards represent something much bigger and deeply personal

Begin by stating how many cards you have put down and then share your thoughts.

When you have finished your partner will reply with a simple statement of "*Thank you for sharing*".

If they would like clarification or to check they have heard everything you wanted to share correctly, they can ask if it's OK to reflect back to you what they understood. Reflection is useful for you as the sharer as it may bring new ideas to mind.

Continue to take turns sharing until you feel complete, or your designated amount of time has elapsed.

The Inner Critic

"You are your own worst critic", the old saying goes. It is true that most people are hard on themselves, you and I included.

There is a critical voice in your head that points out your flaws and mistakes, everyone has one to some degree. This voice is also known as the ego, it's the part of you that is working against you. It is not bad, just intense. The inner critic or ego is the voice within that gives you the choice in every moment whether to choose love or not.

Your inner critic can come out in full force when you are experiencing change, loss or pain. It's that berating voice that shouts in your head when you have the smallest hint of not measuring up in some way. The ego uses time against you, it's the energy of 'If you don't do this immediately something bad will happen to you.' It also makes false promises like 'If you do this, you're going to be rich'.

The voice that says

"You should have done this"

"What a stupid mistake to make"

"You have failed, let down, caused an issue…"

Often your inner critic goes undetected and abuses you under the radar, without conscious awareness. Once you catch yourself saying things that you wouldn't dream of saying to other people, then you can do something about how you speak to yourself. Awareness is key.

I watched as her frustration mounted.

"Come here, come HERE and look at this", she said impatiently, as he continued to play, not paying any attention to what she was saying.

"Come here and look at this picture or I'll tell your Daddy you've been naughty and there's no party." His head swiftly turned to look at his grandma and reluctantly popped himself up onto the sofa to look at the picture she was so adamant he must see.

No sooner had he acquiesced and continued with his own fun, she bellowed again *"Get up off the floor, stop doing that, come here and sit still."*

This grandma was clearly feeling out of control of her little grandson who was waiting eagerly to go into his own 5th birthday party. Whilst it's easy to have an opinion about her 'parenting strategy', watching her was like a reflection of what had been happening in my world the last few days.

My frustration, stemming from fear, had been escalating. Fuelled by a myriad of bombarding thoughts around moving house. A barrage of self-abuse mixed with excitement going on in my head.

"If it's not clean and tidy, they will think I'm a slob."

"If it's not all nicely decorated, they won't see the value and won't want to buy it, then I won't have the money to do...."

I don't know what was going on in grandma's head however I can take a bet that she had some self-deprecation going on around being judged in some way.

My feelings of frustration, helplessness and resistance to what was occurring, spilt out at home as the kids made excuses, moans and groans about tidying their rooms and getting the house prepared for viewings.

A volcano building inside me, heat bubbling away, simmering and occasionally erupting. Thoughts like, *"Why won't they just help? I help them so much and when I need it most, they aren't there for me."* My mind grasping for ways to make them see, to do what I wanted them to do. Panic at the thought of people coming and the house reflecting badly on me.

Then it dawned on me that they were having a different experience around moving than I was. It was the only home they had ever known, their safe haven and sanctuary. Whilst my focus was on a clean slate, a new start and something fresh, their grieving had morphed from losing their dad, to losing their home.

It wasn't that they didn't want to help me, it was they didn't want to move. It was another choice that they did not make. I had confused stubbornness for insubordination and reacted. Once I realised what was going on, I softened. Instead of beating myself up about reacting, I had compassion for myself. It's OK to have times when things are a bit much, when circumstances and feelings are overwhelming. It's an opportunity to learn, grow and begin again.

The main thing I had to give myself compassion for was the use of threats. In my triggered whirlwind of a mind, I felt completely out of control, tossed around and flung up in the air with swirling thoughts. I grasped onto what had been modelled to me. A small voice whispering it was not the best way to approach it and yet the words still flew out of my mouth.

"If you don't help me, don't expect me to help you again with x,y,z".

"If you don't help me, I'll find a two-bedroom house instead of three."

Of course, shouting and threats, didn't work. They dug their heels in even more and what was worse they were now hurt and upset. I took a step back and reached for a better way for all of us. I sat them down and told them the reasons it was important to me for the house to be in a good state. I pointed out the positives of moving and described the bigger picture. I encouraged them by suggesting ways that they could get involved in the process.

After I had some 'buy-in' and a slither of enthusiasm, things changed, they helped with a simple ask. They would come to me with phones in hand showing me pictures of the houses they had been looking at and the desired accessories for their new rooms. Peace reigned in the house now that we were all on the same side again.

When you want someone to do something and they are resistant to it, it can feel very uncomfortable. The trick is to pause, take a step back and be curious about the resistance. An inner ease creates a receptive space for intuitive ideas and feelings to emerge.

Ask yourself, what is this experience or situation showing you? Bring in some love and compassion for yourself and for them. Remember that you care for this person and attempt to view it from their perspective. How is their experience different from yours? How can you meet in the middle?

Shouting only leads to more shouting.

Meet it with calm reasoning and coaxing.

Resistance leads to impatience and resentment.

Meet it with compassion, gentleness and the 'bigger picture'.

If you feel your frustration rising, take a break, breathe and check in on your thoughts. Ensure that you are not being inadvertently driven by negative thoughts and feelings. Take hold of the wheel and get back into the driving seat of your life. Speak directly to the energy. Navigate through the resistance by letting it know your truth.

For example, say out loud or inside your head what you are experiencing.

Argh I feel you, frustration. I feel helpless and at the same time anger building up inside. I feel shaky, out of control. It's not nice feeling like this. I want to feel calmer. I don't know what's come over me. I'd like to figure this out.

Resistance occurs when there is a part of you that feels like it does not deserve the positive shift or change. When in truth, you do deserve all good things. Choose to accept this shift, this change wholeheartedly.

Emotions and regaining power

If your emotions are not acknowledged, expressed or validated, they tend to be buried, stuffed down or swallowed. That doesn't mean that they disappear, instead they swirl around in your body and can make you feel sad, nervous or frustrated. Suppressed emotions often spurt out as irritability which can hurt other people, particularly those closest to you.

If in your childhood or past experiences, you have been discouraged from sharing your feelings or have been shamed for having them, you have most likely learnt to have little tolerance for them. If you missed the emotional training you were ideally meant to receive as a child, then it is likely that you don't have easy access to your emotions. Feelings themselves are not bad or wrong. You cannot choose your feelings. You can choose to connect with them and find out what they are pointing to so that you can respond instead of reacting.

Being in touch with your emotions and feelings gives you more energy, direction and motivation. As you realise that you are not damaged or inadequate in any way, you can start to feel good about yourself. You understand that you are just as valid and important as everyone else. Feeling good about yourself then enables you to stop making yourself small by shrinking and hiding and to take up more space.

Taking up more space can mean making your presence known by speaking up for yourself, being honest and acting. It feels completely different in your body and mind to allow yourself to fully expand and open.

Take 5 Pause and Practice

Star Power Pose

This exercise is a great one for truly experiencing taking up more space and the positive effect it can have on your confidence and self-worth.

Take a seat and bring to mind a thought that causes you frustration or sadness for a moment. Then, cross your arms and legs and allow your forehead to drop down slowly towards your knees, fold your body forward and tuck your chin to your chest.

In this scrunched-up position notice what happens to your thoughts and feelings.

Now unfurl yourself slowly, release your legs so that your feet are firmly placed on the floor, uncross your arms and gently raise your head.

Notice how that posture changes your state- the way your body feels and the quality of your thoughts.

And now, I invite you to stand up. Place your feet hip-width apart, lift your head and look up to the sky. Raise your arms and stretch your hands up to the sky. You are now in a star shape. Turn your lips into a smile and feel the strength, power and space you have created.

Have a go now at thinking about the negative thought from earlier.

You will notice that it is much harder to access.

Take 5 Pause and Action

In the times when you notice a feeling of dread or apprehension wash over you. Pause and tune inwards. Ask yourself "What am I hiding from?", "Am I concealing something?", "Where am I shrinking instead of standing in my power?"

I invite you to stop hiding the real you.

Claim yourself, claim your power, claim your worth.

Inward and Outward Focus

Focusing excessively on your outside world takes you away from what really matters: you.

When you have a habit of wondering what other people are doing, thinking and feeling instead of focusing inward on what you want, believe and feel, then you are giving your power away.

If your emotions were consistently invalidated as a child, you likely developed a pattern of giving away your power. It was your way of ensuring that you received love and care. Being told things *like 'Don't cry or I'll give you something to cry about', 'You don't want that' and 'You don't need that'*, set you up for learning not to trust your choices and feelings. Your decisions were overruled and your power was given to someone else.

When you are used to looking outwards, seeking validation and answers from others, it makes it difficult for you to make your own decisions. Trusting yourself to make the right decisions for you takes practice. Start with small things like, would you like sugar or no sugar in your tea and work up to bigger decisions as you build in confidence. Please be gentle with yourself as you practice, you are learning. We are all a work in progress.

Connecting to your feelings is a wonderful way to deepen your relationship with yourself and others. The more you can connect with your feelings the better you can cultivate a greater compassion and empathy for them. Sharing your feelings about something cuts through the facts and details and gets straight to the heart of what matters. It opens doors and pulls down walls.

Rather than asking lots of questions of yourself and others about the details and facts of a topic, there is a quiet power in helping a person look inward and consider their feelings. To become aware of their intentions, preferences and motivations.

Horizontal and Vertical Question Tool

Horizontal in the general sense refers to physical space from left to right, or space that is parallel to the horizon. Horizontal questions are great for discovering information or facts and things outside of you.

Vertical refers to space from up to down that is perpendicular to the horizon. Vertical questions encourage a focus inward that deepens connection.

When conversing with yourself or someone else, using a mixture of questions helps to open up the conversation. They enable you to discover more about the person or situation than you would have before.

Vertical questions can enliven and light you up because the questions encourage you to consider your values and interests. Being asked to think about things that are important to you helps you to feel considered, heard and validated.

Examples of Vertical and Horizontal Questions

Horizontal	Vertical
Where did you go?	What was the reason for choosing that place?
How are you?	What are you feeling right now?
What happened?	What did you think/feel when that happened?
What did you say?	Why did you say it that way?

Take Back your Power

It is easier than it may seem to give your power away. Parts of you and your energy can be pulled into external situations and other people's stories, dramas and needs without you realising it. When you allow other people's requests, decisions or beliefs to dictate how you feel about yourself, you have given away your power. When you say yes when you want to say no, you give your power away. All these moments and small decisions mount up and you can find yourself becoming very depleted.

This in turn can cause you stress and even resentment as you don't have your full energy and resources at your disposal.

Pulling or drawing yourself back into yourself enables you to claim back your power and stand in your strength. It feels very empowering to feel autonomous and from that space you can act and walk forward with your head held high.

I realised that I was giving my power away by doing too much for other people. Overcompensating, feeling responsible and instead of supporting them, enabling them. I essentially taught them how to treat me by not speaking up, attempting to prevent issues and fighting fires instead of putting them out by proclaiming destructive and unhealthy behaviours.

I wrote in my journal one day:

> *"I need to pull myself back in and realise that it's not healthy to give my power away. To give one man the power over my lovability and self-worth. I will no longer allow someone else's decisions to determine whether I am worthy of love or not. I claim myself. I claim my love."*

The Magic of Words

How you speak to yourself and how other people speak to you has a profound effect. The adage *'sticks and stones may break my bones, but words will never hurt me'* is absolutely not true.

Words are like magic- they can create, and they can destroy.

Using positive words of love, compassion and affirmation creates an environment that encourages care. Negative words of blame, shame and criticism create an environment that encourages suffering and harm.

There are a couple of keywords in your vocabulary that can make a big difference to how you speak to yourself and view situations, they are 'why' and 'but'.

Why?

Asking yourself 'Why?' is the quickest way I am aware of, to spiral yourself down into negative thinking and keep yourself stuck in the past. If you are confused by something or are wondering what has caused a feeling, often the word why will pop up.

Asking why directs your mind to look for answers, unfortunately as you are pre-programmed with a negative bias, the answers are most likely to be negative and self-deprecating.

For example:

Question

"Why did he leave?"

Answer

"Because I didn't try hard enough, wasn't sexy enough, didn't do/ earn/ show enough of......Because he was......"

Asking why? Ties you up in knots because the answer is so subjective, especially if the person or situation is unable or unwilling to give you concrete answers.

A more useful word to use, a far less painful and much more positive one is: how?

How

Asking how questions directed inward with curiosity is a useful way to gain a positive perspective and help you to plan. How questions acknowledge that there is an issue that needs addressing and invites you to be proactive.

Questions emerge from how such as:

- How can I think about what has happened constructively?

- How can I nurture myself through this hard time?
- How can I acknowledge what has happened without placing blame and move forward with grace?

But

But is an interesting little word that can have a negative effect. 'But' in a sentence negates or cancels out what has been said in the previous part of the sentence. It can make a positive comment lose its warmth.

For example,

"I loved the restaurant you took me to, but the music was too loud."

The complimentary sentence started off so well and yet by using 'but' in the middle and continuing with a negative conclusion, the whole sentence has lost its sparkle and original intent.

Yes, but...

Perhaps a friend has spent time sharing something heartfelt, intending to guide you. Then when they have finished sharing you say "Yes, but." That is the kind of response that makes the recipient's heart sink a little. It is like saying "I have been listening however I don't agree". It is not additive, it is subtractive.

But, but, but

But can also play in your mind as a negative mantra and you can find yourself doing the 'but' song that sounds like an engine attempting to start and backfiring, unable to move.

But I can't...

But what if....

But how will I....

The remedy to but is and.

And

The little word 'and' can make a huge difference in a sentence, transforming it from subtractive to additive. From negative to positive. Using 'and' in a sentence enables you to include more detail and information. To deepen awareness.

The mindful intention of using 'and' instead of 'but' can transform the way you speak to yourself and reply to other people.

Let's take the previous 'but' sentence example and use 'and' as a replacement.

"I loved the restaurant you took me to, but the music was too loud."

"I loved the restaurant you took me to and next time I would like to try out a quieter sort of ambience."

And for "Yes, but"

An alternative could be

"I have taken onboard what you have said, thank you and I agree with x, y. z points and yet I am still confused by...."

Dr. Emoto and the wonders of Water

I was first introduced to the effect of language on your mind and body when I came across the wonderful work of internationally acclaimed water researcher Dr. Masaru Emoto. Dr. Emoto conducted experiments with water crystals, the results of which are captivating and thought-provoking. He took samples of water and exposed them to words, pictures and music, both positive and negative. He then froze the water and looked at the crystal formations they made.

When he offered words like love, gratitude, beautiful, peace and joy, the resulting crystal patterns were beautiful and intricate. When Dr. Emoto offered negative words, such as hate, ugly, loathing, inadequate and abhorrent, the resulting crystals were unstructured and blob-like.

If you consider that your body is made up of at least 65% water and then consider the effects that words have on water, it can be a revelation. It's knowledge which may encourage you to use your words towards yourself and others with careful intention. To use more words of love as these experiments showed human thoughts and intentions can physically alter the molecular structure of water.

Your body is composed of upwards of 100 trillion cells and the more harmonious the vibrations in your body are, the healthier the body and mind is.

Take 5 Pause and Action

Write your favourite positive words of affirmation or terms of endearment such as love, beauty, and joy and place them around a bottle of water or underneath a glass of water and allow the vibration of the words to infuse the water. Then drink the water.

This is a lovely way of adding positive and loving vibrations to your body and mind. As well as acting as a reminder to speak kindly to yourself and others.

13

THE DRAMA TRIANGLE

TAKING A CLOSE LOOK AT YOUR RELATIONSHIPS TO DETERMINE whether they are healthy or not is an important and courageous exercise. Even more so when you examine your role within them. It's common not to be consciously aware of how unhealthy, unproductive or toxic your relationships have become. Issues can creep up over time little by little without being detected or recognised.

Having an awareness of the drama triangle helps you to understand how you naturally respond to situations where you are attempting to get your needs met in unhealthy ways. Like me, you may not have been aware until now that your behaviours are inadvertently causing you additional suffering. By bidding for connection and support in specific unhealthy ways you are likely to be stepping into certain 'roles' that continue the drama and pain.

This knowledge helps you to step out of the drama by recognising when you fall into a role and then choosing not to engage. This reduces the number of times you will find yourself feeling powerless and helpless. You will see the 'drama baton' being offered to you, be able to recognise it and choose not to pick it up.

The drama triangle is a model that describes how conflict arises between people, often in intense interactions where there is an unmet need. When in the drama people will adopt one or more of the roles to try and control the situation and swing it in their favour. It was devised by Dr Stephen Karpman in 1968. The model has 3 roles that people participate in; the victim, rescuer and persecutor.

The Victim Role

This is the person who feels helpless or powerless, like they can never get ahead in life. They often think things like *"This always happens to me"*, *"Everyone's against me"*, *"It's not my fault"* and *"That's not fair."*

They can be defensive and unempathetic because their feelings are more important to them than other people's. They refuse to accept any responsibility for their situation often denying their role in it, no matter how small it may be. A simple *'yes, hands up that was me'* in these situations would go such a long way in defusing the tension.

They will give little or no effort and yet suggest that they have tried everything without success. They will often say *"Yes, but…"* when others offer a solution to a problem, this response is invalidating and dismissive.

They are the glass-half-empty people who believe that the world is against them, not for them. They will use countless excuses, dramatic language and body expressions to emphasise their made-up unfortunate circumstances. They find very little joy in life.

They can be ultra-sensitive to the most basic and harmless feedback and take it as a personal attack. They will defend themselves veraciously, sometimes going on the counterattack. Victims attempt to rally people around them to agree with their cause. They can be very ambiguous with their statements and go back and forth in making decisions which can be incredibly confusing.

Healing the Victim Role

Consider and appreciate what you do have control over.

Think like a problem solver.

Look at yourself as a survivor, someone who is resilient.

156

The Rescuer Role

This is the person who takes responsibility for other people's problems and makes them their own. Whilst at the same time they are not looking closely at their own lives which could be out of balance.

They say things like *"I'm nice, I'll help them."* Or *"If they just did what I say, they'd be happy."*

The rescuer wants to solve your problems and take on a caretaking role. However, if the help is not warranted or asked for, they may use guilt tactics to meet their needs. This can lead to resentment. The rescuer seeks out some sort of benefit from their efforts and if this is not forthcoming, you may hear them say things such as *"After all I've done for you, and this is how you treat me"*.

The rescuer has similarities to a 'peacekeeper' (which is not part of the drama triangle) although the concept can overlap. Whilst the peacekeeper is more inclined to do what it takes for the conflict to end, to have a positive resolution and harmony. The rescuer requires some sort of prize.

Healing the Rescuer Role

Support instead of rescue- learn to become more of a teacher or a coach.

Stop the self-abandonment.

Learn to value yourself and take steps to increase your self-worth.

The Persecutor Role

The persecutor is the person who is frustrated, they are self-righteous and tend to be a bit of a bully. Generally, the 'know it all' and the smartest cookie in the room. They are not shy about telling you how they think it is.

The persecutor criticises the enabling behaviours of the rescuer and blames the victim. They will shout from the mountain tops how much it is your fault and blame you for not following their way of doing things. They are the "I told you so" type, standing berating whilst shaking their heads in contempt.

They may think or say things like *"They're wrong and I'm right"* and *"They need to do what I say."* They want to keep the victim down and focus on being right as they fear becoming a victim themselves. They can be controlling, disrespectful and nasty. They offer no real solutions to the problem as they stay up on their high horse.

Healing the Persecutor Role

Challenge instead of criticising.

Encourage people instead of discouraging.

Have some patience and grace.

Take 5 Pause and Journal

After an encounter that has left you with unmet needs and feeling powerless, take some time to reflect on the experience. Take your mind back and observe yourself, like a fly on the wall.

Ask yourself the following questions and write down your thoughts as honestly as possible. Being honest with yourself will create greater awareness and more opportunities for healing.

- ♥ What was your role in the interaction?
- ♥ Did you change roles throughout the interaction between victim, rescuer and persecutor?
- ♥ What value did the role(s) bring to you?

♥ What actions can you now take? What limits or boundaries can you put in place?

♥ Do you find it difficult to say no? If so, practice saying no daily and write about how building up your 'no' muscle feels over 21 days.

Me, The Recovering Rescuer

I recognise myself most in the rescuer role. My first response to my husband leaving was an attempt to rescue him from himself. To me he seemed sad and lost and I felt a compulsion to help. I truly thought that if I didn't attempt to help, that I was abandoning him and that would be going against my marriage vows.

I remember countless times when I would offer solutions to solve his reasons for leaving, attempting to 'show' him a better way. I truly thought I could convince him that the 'grass is greener where you water it' and that it was best for him to stay with me and our children.

What I didn't understand then was that I was allowing myself to be harmed in the name of love. In my misplaced understanding of love and commitment. I poured my love and energy into the potential. My whole perception of our marriage was built on hope, hope that 'love' would prevail. Hope that things would get better. Hope that he would show me the warmth he once did. Hope that I could get through with my words somehow. Now I know that this isn't love, the quality of true, tender love that is available to us all.

It wasn't until I stopped attempting to rescue him that two major learnings arose within me. Firstly, people must find their own way in life. The optimal way for them to learn is through their own choices and decisions and grow based on their own life experiences. I wasn't helping by being the constant emotional blanket, cheerleader and problem solver.

Secondly, once I reclaimed my energy and stopped abandoning myself, I understood that I had been giving away far too much of my own energy. I had not been looking at how unhappy I had become, how helpless I felt, how much I craved emotional connection. By focusing outside of myself and how to hold onto my marriage, I had completely missed the fact I was participating in the role of 'rescuing' to my detriment.

There were still the occasional times when I would get confused, fall back or get sucked into the rescuer role, feeling guilty about saying no and putting myself first. I had to remind myself over and over again that self-preservation is a right. That just because someone engaged with me, I did not have to entertain them. I could stop tip-toeing around the feelings of someone who stamped all over mine and allow my heart to be heard.

The greatest gift you can give to yourself is self-love and self-compassion. When you love yourself, exactly as you are, it is much more difficult for anyone to manipulate you or get under your skin.

For example, when I received texts months after we had separated that seemed sincere about wanting to talk, had an interest in me, or came with a hint of sadness, my resolve would weaken. I felt awkward and uneasy about upholding my boundaries and not re-engaging with someone who deeply hurt me and was no longer healthy for me. Once I understood the drama triangle, I was able to gain clarity and my resolve became a tower of strength.

Once I was able to see the games being played, I stepped out of the triangle. I felt no need to rescue, feel victimised or persecute. Instead, I chose to have compassion for myself, and all concerned and not give the situation any more of my precious energy.

When different layers of learning and healing appear now, perhaps triggered by a song, a random memory or a comment, I focus on acceptance and forgiveness. Acceptance and forgiveness are two choices that will need to be made, repeatedly until there are no more layers to heal. No more waves appearing in your usually calm emotional seas. I am mindful now to remember the lesson and not disappointments.

Part 4

LET YOUR LOVE SHINE

14

LOVE

"Love is patient, love is kind. It does not envy, it does not boast, it is not proud. It does not dishonour others, it is not self-seeking, it is not easily angered, it keeps no record of wrongs. Love does not delight in evil but rejoices with the truth. It always protects, always trusts, always hopes, always perseveres."

– Bible, Corinthians 13:5

LOVE IS YOUR CORE NATURE.

You are love incarnate.

I believe you come from love, you are love, you return to love, and in the middle, you can choose love.

Love is what sustains you, it is the soil you're planted in and the oxygen that fills your lungs.

Sometimes you can forget that you are loved and need to be reminded. Sometimes that reminder can be quite unexpected, a rude awakening that jolts you back into awareness. Other times it is gentle and nurturing like a warm summer breeze wafting across your face.

There's a saying *"we see the world not as it is, but as we are"*. When you choose to see with love, you will see that the world is filled with love.

163

Once you see that you are surrounded by love it becomes more and more uncomfortable to choose anything but love.

How do you let love in?

If somewhere along the line you had to protect yourself from hurt and pain, you may have closed your heart to truly feeling love again. You may now find it hard to let love in, even for yourself. When you are not able to feel love, it makes you feel separate and isolated. Love is a gift for everyone including you. It's your right to be connected to love and to bask in its warm embrace.

So, how do you let love in? The answer is to start with yourself. I believe that the best love stories are the ones not about our lovers but the tales of how we found ourselves. Ask yourself, Am I appreciating who I am? How much of what I express is so that someone else will like me? Who would I be if I didn't feel the need to hide, protect or defend?

It's not the situation you find yourself in that matters most, it's how you feel about yourself. You can absolutely still feel good about yourself whilst the world around you is throwing eggs. You can stand tall, be firm in your resolve and hold healthy boundaries. A tool I like to use is to imagine a sheet of clear plastic in front of you and every time an accusation, angry or hurtful words are thrown at you, see them as eggs splatting against the plastic and observe them running down, not touching you, not harming you.

How do I know how to let love in?

How can I stand steadfastly in this truth?

I know it from personal experience. I know that it is an absolute choice and the rewards for choosing love, to let love in are huge. I have learnt that to connect with people it's necessary to express my vulnerabilities.

I've discovered that when you intend to live in a loving way, to make decisions guided by love, it isn't always easy or immediately obvious how to go about it. It is a choice. It does not depend on your circumstances. It does not have to be an easy choice or the most obvious. You can make the choice no matter what is going on around you, for you. That's when the magic starts to happen.

I believed that choosing love meant upholding my marriage vows, and continuing to live by them, even when my husband did not. I discovered that choosing to love meant giving myself permission to accept love, to invite it in, for me. I chose to love me, for me. I decided to trust that I am lovable. I allowed what 'is', to be enough. Not out of obligation, not out of greed or selfishness, simply out of love for me.

The rewards for making the choice surprised me. I was enlivened, filled up from the inside. This invigorated and brightened my life, appearing in many large and small ways. From the kindness of a lady at the supermarket who helped me out when I was 10p short for my shopping, to saying no to the old version of me. When I chose to let love in, my whole world opened. A whole new world of possibilities, full of hope and faith, in myself and my future life.

It was like shedding my old self to reveal the new me. In choosing love, I chose to let go of my old identity and create a new one. I no longer identified with the version of me that would tolerate being emotionally neglected, being told I wasn't good enough or doing enough and avoiding rocking the boat. I created a new map of my values and beliefs, guided by love and a strong resolve.

I was released from the confusion that I often felt which left me feeling small and unsure of myself. Confusion from words and behaviours that kept me down, stopping me from working out the truth of the situation, that I could choose an alternative- true love for myself, love born out of respect.

I was released from being grateful for the crumbs I received when I deserved the whole cake. I didn't even realise at the time I was settling for so much less than life and love wanted for me. I gained clarity in my mind and peace in my heart, which felt like a soft fluffy cloud where there was once a heavy storm cloud.

I gained a beautiful internal recognition, stemming from my heart and then radiating out like rays of the sun beaming outwards into my whole being and beyond. Recognition that felt like a warm cosy hug that said I can trust myself, that I can believe in myself and that I am fundamentally OK. An understanding that I have a lot to give and deserve all good things.

Love gives me a sense of pride that I am living life with integrity and grace.

Love gives me hope of continuously creating a meaningful and purposeful life where I achieve what I set out to do.

Love gives me faith that what's for me will not pass me by.

What gets in the way?

It is especially tricky when you have spent quite some time rising from situations that have pulled you down. When you have worked courageously through blood, sweat and tears. Clawed yourself out of a black hole of grief, loss and despair, to find that the situation or behaviour that you have gained clarity on, forgiven and started to move on from rears its head again.

It comes in the form of flattery.

It comes in the form of playing on your kindness.

It comes in the form of offers of assistance.

It may manifest as an attempt to find that slither of doubt and confusion to hook into. A ploy to claim back or bask under your shining light.

In these times remember:

Love is patient, love is kind.

Love encourages you to have patience and kindness, for yourself and the situation. You are a work in progress as are we all. There may be moments where you may question yourself and that's OK. There may be moments where you feel anger or frustration bubble up from your newfound contentment and that's OK too. These moments are fleeting and if you allow yourself to let them flow, they will dissipate. Avoid grasping, pushing away or holding onto emotions, simply acknowledge them and let them float away.

It keeps no record of wrongs

Holding onto old stories and hurts and perhaps even using them against someone is harmful to you. It is not in alignment and integrity with who you are. Whilst you have likely lived through painful experiences, holding onto them to use as ammunition later takes up far too much precious space within you. Other people can sense resentment, anger and blame coming from you like a bad smell. You cannot hide it no matter how much you try to disguise it with nice scents in the form of flattery or disingenuous words.

Practising forgiveness is a wonderful antidote to any poison within you that is waiting to be dispensed. Forgiveness is for you. Forgiveness is a choice, not a feeling. It is facing the wrongs done to you, recognising the emotions inside and choosing not to hold it against the other person. Forgiveness allows you to take the poison out of the situation. It doesn't necessarily stop you from remembering. It does enable you to make peace with it so that it is not front and centre in your mind anymore. No longer chewing you up, stirring your mind and emotions. It helps you to step out of the whirlwind around you and see it objectively for what it is.

From a place of calm and peace the feeling of retribution is difficult to muster. Thus, giving you more space, more bandwidth to concentrate on self-love and compassion. Forgiveness is a process that you will need to come back to often. It's a normal part of the healing process to keep forgiving the same hurt, sometimes daily.

Love does not delight in evil but rejoices with the truth

You know the truth of a situation, even if it starts with a subtle knowing from deep inside you and gains traction as you discover more information. You know the truth from your gut feeling, your intuition. If something feels 'off', then it's off!

When you have been bruised in life, emotions are likely to be a factor in your decision-making. In fact, most decisions are based on emotions from the car you drive, the house you live in and the amount of personal access you give to someone. Utilising truth enables you to make judgements and decisions without relying on emotion alone. To look at the facts first.

You can have compassion for a situation or person and still be unwavering in your resolve. It helps to have the facts in front of you that are as clear as day. If you find yourself wobbling when you have remained strong, I encourage you to revisit the facts of the situation and the actions a person took. Not the words that they said that may have been designed to get an emotional response- the cold, hard facts.

It always protects, always trusts, always hopes, always perseveres.

Love protects you by making the act of being dishonoured uncomfortable. Love has no tricks and does not attempt to pull the wool over your eyes. Love is pure, true and honest. Love encourages you to trust yourself above all others. It gives you the flexibility to know when to trust someone and when to be discerning.

It always hopes for the best whilst being prepared for life to challenge your perceptions and expectations. It always perseveres by showing you that you are loved that you are Love and that you are worthy of its perseverance.

Loving and liking are not synonymous

Instead of focusing your energy on the loss of a relationship that wasn't as deep as you thought it was, where there were conflicting values, lack of compatibility or involved abuse, you can choose to nurture and cultivate the most important relationships in your life now. And while keeping the door open for new ones.

You can have love for someone, the same kind of love you hold for all sentient beings and not like them anymore. You can choose who you are friends with. You can be friendly towards another person without being their friend. You can treat others with respect, even when they do not offer you the same.

Take 5 Pause and Practice

Gently release the cords that connected you

Guided meditation involving imagery is a very effective way of gently releasing energy that is not healthy for you to hold onto. The following meditation is a version of cord-cutting. It transforms the energy around a person or situation allowing more space for healing and growth.

Releasing The Cords That Bind

Find a comfortable and upright posture

Take some deep centring breaths

Close your eyes and imagine sitting at the edge of a body of water at sunset. It could be the sea or a lake with a dock.

Feel the peace and calm wash over you as you take some deep releasing breaths.

Look out over the vast body of water and know that this chapter in your life is a mere drop or ripple and that there is so much more available to you.

As you scan your surroundings start to focus on something that has caught your eye and notice that it is a wooden boat tied up to a post.

As the boat bobs up and down on the gentle waves, consider what causes waves in your mind and emotions. What or who makes large waves that knock you off your course, off-centre?

Make the choice now to place into the boat anything or anyone that no longer serves your highest good. Decide that it is now time to release them with love.

Imagine filling up the boat until it is ready for its next journey, its next adventure with its passengers and cargo safe and happy inside.

You can see the passengers' faces and they are relaxed, there is no resistance or animosity around journeying onwards without you. They know it is best for all concerned.

Take hold of the rope that is securing the boat to the post and unwind the loops. As you unwind the rope, slowly releasing it from the post, acknowledge and give thanks for all the ways these threads of connection have benefited you.

Once the boat has been released from the post, place the rope inside the boat and allow it to float away.

Watch the boat as it floats further and further away from you, as it does so you notice that you feel lighter and lighter with a sense of freedom.

Watch the boat get closer and closer to the horizon as the sunset fades to dusk. The boat disappearing into the fading light.

Take some deep releasing breaths, knowing all is well. That part of your journey is now complete, and the passengers and cargo of the boat are free to also embark on their own separate journeys too.

Wiggle your fingers and wiggle your toes.

Gently blink open your eyes and come back into the room.

Notice what has changed, notice what is different.

15

SOFTEN

"The trick to doing this is to stay with emotional distress without tightening into aversion, to let fear soften us rather than harden into resistance."

-Pema Chodron

"Give them back", Iris shouted, the usual sibling argument was *occurring upstairs or so it seemed.*

"Give them back Alfie" she shrilled, this time her voice cracked a little which caught my attention. I was in the middle of a task that required my concentration, and these outbursts were distracting me. Already feeling fragile, I was frustrated at having to put down what I was doing so that peace could reign again in the house.

As I reached the top of the stairs, I found both my children having a tug of war with a single white Nike sock. I could see and hear that Iris was getting more frustrated with her brother as he continued to hold onto the sock, somewhat bemused by her reaction and nonetheless determined to win.

"Just give her the sock back please" I said to Alfie as he let go. Iris, clearly distressed and overwhelmed from the exertion, shouted that "he shouldn't take her things" and ran away crying.

Still somewhat irritated by the whole drama I had a chat with Alfie and then went to find Iris. I thought I'd find her in her bedroom, but she wasn't there. I checked my bedroom, the living room, the den and garden and she was nowhere to be seen. At that point I got a bit worried and concerned. She was clearly upset by more than the loss of a single sock.

I called out her name- silence.

Then out of the corner of my eye I saw something move in my walk-in wardrobe, the doors were slightly ajar. There she was my beautiful girl, curled up in the corner, sobbing her heart out. Sat in a ball with her knees bent up, her arms folded together and her head resting on top of them. My heart sank to my toes as I could sense the pain, she was in.

All of the frustration and tension I had, the thoughts about the kids wasting my time melted away instantly. Being replaced with love, concern and compassion. I softened.

I opened the door, and she looked up at me, tears rolling down her anguished face. She unfolded her arms and held them out to me as I knelt in front of her and took her in my arms. I held her close and sat with her until she felt better. I understood that her deeper suffering was the loss of her dad, that she felt that life as she knew it had been taken away from her. She was holding onto the sock because she didn't want the pain and distress of anything else being taken from her.

This experience, taking the time to slow down, to feel into and connect with what was going on and with my children was poignant. It deepened our relationship at a really stressful and hard time for all of us. I chose to soften instead of hardening. To seek to open my heart instead of close it. To stay with the pain and to understand it until it was no longer something to be feared. To hold space for emotions to flow for the benefit of myself and my children.

Choice Point

When you have been hurt, betrayed or let down you have a choice; let hurt harden you or let hurt soften you. There's a saying *"boiling water can soften potatoes and harden an egg"*. It's a testament to your character as to how you chose to respond when life heats up to boiling point.

You have the choice to allow the hurt and pressure to be utilised in a positive way. To soften in your response, in heart and mind.

Take 5 Pause and Practice

Soften Exercise

Remember that reading something offers one level of awareness, whilst practising or doing something really helps you to embed the learning. I invite you to take a pause, to put away or minimise any distractions and to be present in the moment.

Place your feet on the ground and sit in a comfortable, upright and alert position. Relax your shoulders and jaw and take a few deep belly breaths. Then have a go at the practice offered below.

Soften Mantra

When you notice that you are being hard on yourself or a situation, a useful mantra to refocus your thoughts is *'soften'*. The word itself repeated slowly several times can encourage a softening of tension in your body and to bring awareness of any negativity or criticism that is swirling around your mind.

Repeat the word **Soften** slowly and softly

Soften

Notice the images that pop up in your mind

Soften

Notice the warmth that radiates out from your heart

Soften

Notice how your body takes a big deep breath

Soften

Notice how your shoulders release and your jaw relaxes

Soften

Notice the peaceful sensation that washes over your body and mind.

When an experience is difficult, you can fight with it. In the moment, your natural instincts are likely to tell you to be hard, to put up your walls and close your heart. What if instead you surrender to it? Let down your walls, and be open to the experience? You will grow from the pain by giving up the hard walls you have surrounded yourself with and softening your heart and mind to what comes your way.

Learning to relax with life, to go with the flow rather than against the current and to see what happens from a place of softness, enables you to make decisions with more wisdom. To take actions with more power than if you were fighting. Remember when you are in a calm, balanced state you have access to all your resources, as opposed to when your system is stressed and shut down.

Consider what would softening look like in this moment?

What could result from softening?

Who might you become?

Soften Practice

Make a tight fist. Now soften your hand and let it open and expand.

Repeat making a fist and this time notice the sensation of release, relaxation and unfurling. Notice the lightness, the sensation of unfolding and expansion. Imagine it like a flower bud opening.

Now do the same with your neck and shoulders, just for a moment. Raise your shoulders towards your ears and tighten them. Feel how compressed your whole body becomes. And release the tightness, slowly and gently. Notice how much more space and openness has been created.

Without adding more tension this time, simply ask for another level of relaxation and unwinding in your shoulders. Notice how you feel emotionally when you do this.

Soften Acronym

Acronyms are a great way to remember the essence of an idea. I hope you find this one useful to remember the importance of softening.

S- suffering

O- open up

F- face it

T- tell yourself a different story

E- empathy

N- notice

Slow down and notice your suffering

Something causes you to experience fear or hurt that creates suffering. It could be a comment someone has made, a negative experience or a fear about the future. Your likely first reaction is to want to shut down, to tighten up, to make it go away. The invitation here is to slow down and to notice that you are suffering. To take a moment to feel that fear. To notice that you want to 'harden' in order to protect yourself.

How do you know that you are suffering if you don't give yourself the opportunity to slow down long enough to recognise it?

John Lennon is quoted as saying *"Life is what happens whilst you're busy doing other things."*

Life is a gift and by attempting to bypass suffering, you are inadvertently missing out on the treasures it is offering you. Sitting with your pain and suffering long enough to listen to and understand what it is telling you, is valuable.

By slowing down, you allow yourself to simply be- you are after all a 'human being' not a human 'doing'

Open Up

Instead of hardening, choose to open up to the emotions that are causing you fear and discomfort. Open to kindness, compassion and love. Opening to something involves letting it in. To expand rather than contract. Like unlocking a door and opening it to reveal what is on the other side. Opening involves a level of courage and vulnerability. To explore the unknown. Notice how your body feels. Is it tense and contracted or is it open and relaxed? Notice what thoughts are playing in your mind. Are they positive and light or are they negative and heavy?

Consider what 'opens you up', what kinds of thoughts, feelings, experiences and sensations enable you to expand? Could it be the sound of a child laughing? Watching spring lambs playing? An elderly couple walking down the street arm in arm? When you open your heart, you will sense it as a warm glow in your chest, like a big sunshine radiating out of your heart space.

Face It

Once you allow yourself to notice the scary thoughts, you can face them and explore them. You can begin to unpick the fear and see it for what it is. To perceive it from a different angle. Where before it seemed large and looming, in the light of awareness, what you were afraid of is likely to be smaller than you imagined.

There are several acronyms for the word fear.

FEAR- false evidence appearing real

FEAR- forget everything and run

FEAR- face everything and rise

Whilst forgetting everything and running may seem at first like an appealing option, it doesn't solve anything. Facing your fear, looking at it square in the eyes and not removing your gaze until it isn't daunting anymore enables you to rise above it.

Use the concept of false evidence appearing real to help you. Ask yourself some questions to uncover any potential masks this fear has been hiding behind. Can you disprove or add doubt to the thoughts that wanted to remain rigid?

Beliefs are only thoughts that you have said or heard many times over and have been made true. The word belief has 'lie' in the middle- where then can you find the lie? Asking yourself questions like- Is it really true? What proof do I have? Where's the evidence? enables you to see beliefs, thoughts and situations from different perspectives and therefore relaxing their grip on you.

Tell yourself a different story

You can gain insights into your own suffering by noticing the thoughts you are thinking and the stories you are telling yourself. Are you spending time worrying and making up stories in your mind about what may happen? Or reliving something unpleasant from the past? In an anxious state you may get stuck in the details, and get carried away with the negative feelings and so to attempt to feel better you drift away into a fantasy, story or planning. That approach seems to offer comfort and the promise of feeling more secure. Yet it can often serve to dig you deeper into suffering.

The good news is that you can put those stories down, choose to leave them alone, allow them to fade away and then tell yourself a different story. Focus on one that is more empowering, kind and compassionate.

Where can you change the narrative?

When telling yourself reasons to be angry, hurt or closed down, what can you now say to bring in compassion?

Rather than telling yourself that you were wrong, foolish, duped. Tell the story of wanting to see the best in someone. That you trusted until you were given reason to create healthier boundaries.

Instead of judgment, blame or shame, where can you replace your thoughts, words and stories with kindness, forgiveness and understanding?

Empathy

Empathy is walking in someone else's shoes to find out how a situation felt or was experienced. To understand it from their point of view, rather than your own. This skill generates curiosity, to listen with the intention of understanding and with an open mind. Acknowledge and validate the feelings involved by saying phrases like *"I'm sorry you are going through this"*. Use empathy as an opportunity to learn something about yourself, the other person or the situation that you were not aware of before.

Be sure that you are using empathy and not sympathy. A psychology tutor once told me a story about the difference between the two which has really stuck with me.

A man was walking along and came across a deep hole, he heard a boy shouting for help. As he peered over the side, he could see the boy encased, trapped at the bottom with no way out. The man jumps into the hole and reassures him. He feels sorry for the boy and yet he is no real help to him because now he is in the same predicament. This is sympathy.

A lady comes along the path and hears the cries for help from the man and the boy. She peers into the hole and sees them both at the bottom. She wants to help and understands that they are scared. She looks around and finds some rope, ties it to a tree and throws down the rope to the man and boy. They use the rope to pull themselves out and at the top she listens to their ordeal and offers them a cuppa. This is empathy.

Notice

Now that you have taken a moment to slow down and acknowledge something scary that is causing suffering, opened to the sensations and faced the fear, eye to eye. Then told yourself a different story whilst bringing in empathy. You are now invited to put it all together and notice the change.

What do you notice that is different now?

Energy follows focus. Or another way to say this is your energy flows where your attention goes. For example, if you put your attention on your feet that's where your energy goes, and you notice all the sensations in your feet such as warmth and tingling. Have a go and notice.

What has changed?

What feelings, thoughts, and sensations are different now through practising the process of soften?

How have these new insights given you nourishment? Food for thought to help you grow and prosper?

Write down in your journal or notepad any insights or 'Aha' moments that you would benefit from remembering.

16

9 STAR KI YEARS- EVERYTHING IN GOOD TIME

Nine Stages of Transformation

When you have been through a big change and life seems uncertain, knowing that the phase you are in will not last indefinitely can be comforting. Knowing that there is a plan, a structure that you can use as a guiding light or North Star, offers a sense of assurance.

Each year of the nine-year cycle brings a different focus. A different theme. A chance to learn and grow in nine different areas from potential to full steam ahead. Being aware of and intentionally working with the theme of the year enables you to use time to your advantage, to ride the wave.

The theme of each year supports planning ahead and offers insight into the types of experiences you are likely to have, including emotionally. Having an awareness of what you are stepping into can be very helpful. If you know what you'll likely encounter, what to expect and the energy behind it, it makes life so much easier. You can rest into it, like allowing yourself to be supported in the arms of a comfy sofa and wrapped up in a warm cosy blanket. Occasionally you may need to adjust, get some water and have a stretch and yet overall, you feel assured.

Each year has a metaphorical season associated with it, which carries certain qualities and imagery. It is a cycle so you can use it to understand where you have been, where you are now and where you are going.

I have provided the dates for your next two 9-year cyclic themes in the following pages. To discover subsequent years simply add 9. For example, if your birth number is 1 Water and you're in the year 2023, the theme of the year is strategy. This theme will then reoccur in 2032, 2041, 2050, 2059 and so on.

One Year: Potential/ Dreaming

Observe and dream

If your birth number is One:	2022, 2031
If your birth number is Two:	2021, 2030
If your birth number is Three:	2020, 2029
If your birth number is Four:	2019, 2028
If your birth number is Five:	2018, 2027
If your birth number is Six:	2017, 2026
If your birth number is Seven:	2016, 2025
If your birth number is Eight:	2015, 2024
If your birth number is Nine:	2014, 2023

The One Year invites you to slow down, go within and spend time in reflection, prayer and meditation. This year is associated with the energy of winter where it seems like nothing is growing when actually the seeds are soaking up rich nutrients in preparation for spring. It can be a very nourishing time to gestate, receive and deepen your connection with yourself and the source of Life. This is a great year to learn, develop a skill and study, to allow yourself time to imagine and dream about what you can create in future months and years.

Things will not happen quickly this year, so be prepared for some frustration and opportunities for patience. Your intuition will be greatly heightened this year. You may encounter lessons that enable you to take back your personal power and discover who you are. Your intuition will help you make decisions from love not fear.

This year is a chance to explore lifelong beliefs around your value and worth and to find a deeper more meaningful love for yourself. You may have experiences that dissolve old ways of doing things that no longer serve you so that you can become the best version of yourself. To encourage your authentic self to surface more and more.

Two Year: Strategy

Plan and nurture

If your birth number is One:	2023, 2032
If your birth number is Two:	2022, 2031
If your birth number is Three:	2021, 2030
If your birth number is Four:	2020, 2029
If your birth number is Five:	2019, 2028
If your birth number is Six:	2018, 2027
If your birth number is Seven:	2017, 2026
If your birth number is Eight:	2016, 2025
If your birth number is Nine:	2015, 2024

After the reflection and dreaming of the One Year, the Two Year is all about building the foundations for the future. You may feel like things have stagnated however this pause is a chance to connect, practice patience and plan. This year is associated with the energy of late summer. It's that quiet period between noon and 3 pm, a favourite time for a little nap.

A Two Year is a good time to get your ducks in a row and create a strategy. Decide on the ideal ways you want to show up and serve. Once you have decided on a way ahead, look out for mentors or people offering support and help. This is a year where helpers are likely to show up in serendipitous ways.

Whilst you are in this period of 'downtime', it's a great opportunity to consider any obstructions in your life. What interferes with everything going smoothly? Ensure that you give from your overflow and maintain healthy boundaries during this year. It's a really good time to consider what makes you feel truly loved and nurtured. If you are not balanced around nurturing ask yourself, how can I receive more? Turn love inward and enjoy the things in life that bring you comfort and pleasure. Have a massage or a spa day, go on your favourite hike, eat delicious food and bring the family together.

Get everything prepared and think through your plans as next year it's time for lift-off!

Three Year: Let's Go

Rise and proceed

If your birth number is One:	2015, 2024
If your birth number is Two:	2014, 2023
If your birth number is Three:	2022, 2031
If your birth number is Four:	2021, 2030
If your birth number is Five:	2020, 2029
If your birth number is Six:	2019, 2028
If your birth number is Seven:	2018, 2027
If your birth number is Eight:	2017, 2026
If your birth number is Nine:	2016, 2025

This is a year of new possibilities fuelled by the energy of sunrise and springtime, symbolic of new growth and development. After the planning stages of the last two years (1 Water and 2 Earth), you can now start to put those plans into action. Ideas are springing up like the emergence of new shoots in spring. It's a year of vibrant, rising energy. Lots of ideas will be popping up in your mind and not all of them will make the distance. Like a plethora of baby sea turtles clambering from the beach to the sea, many will make it however not all.

The slower pace of the last two years is replaced by enthusiasm, and you will feel impulsive and confident. Be fearless, and try new things. With such rapid progress, being successful in your endeavours will require you to keep an eye on the details and remain focused on your goals.

A perfect year to initiate a new project or to go on an adventure. Give things a go and get feedback from them. If it doesn't work, move forward onto the next idea. Don't get stuck in stagnation or overthinking. Your enthusiasm will be an inspiration to others. Remember with all this activity to slow down now and then, give yourself time to relax, perhaps on a Sunday afternoon.

Four Year: Growth

Rapid growth and development

If your birth number is One:	2016, 2025
If your birth number is Two:	2015, 2024
If your birth number is Three:	2023, 2032
If your birth number is Four:	2022, 2031
If your birth number is Five:	2021, 2030
If your birth number is Six:	2020, 2029
If your birth number is Seven:	2019, 2028
If your birth number is Eight:	2018, 2027
If your birth number is Nine:	2017, 2026

This is the second year in a two-year cycle of growth and change that started last year in your Three Year. Now that your ideas have pushed through and made the distance, it's time to cultivate them into projects. It's time to flesh out your ideas and take the next steps. Ideally its best to stay focussed on the general direction you started last year, to build on it. Persevere and do not "throw in the towel" if you hit any roadblocks.

Staying focused may prove to be tricky at times as this year the direction that you thought you were heading in can suddenly change. It can feel like an uncertain time where you are indecisive and unsure, like everything is up in the air. You may even have the rug pulled out from under you in some way. An image for the 4 Tree is wind and so this energy can feel like it's blowing you around and even off course.

Know though that wonderful things are happening this year, sometimes the wind needs to shake things up a little to get you on the right path. Avoid impulsive actions or procrastination and develop a practice of compassion and patience with yourself. Stay grounded and get some advice where needed. This year you can be influential as well as influenced, elders or wise people are likely to show up and help.

Five Year: In the centre

Pause and Balance

If your birth number is One:	2017, 2026
If your birth number is Two:	2016, 2025
If your birth number is Three:	2015, 2024
If your birth number is Four:	2023, 2032
If your birth number is Five:	2022, 2031
If your birth number is Six:	2021, 2030
If your birth number is Seven:	2020, 2029
If your birth number is Eight:	2019, 2028
If your birth number is Nine:	2018, 2027

In a 5 Earth year it can feel like everything is coming towards you all at once. Experiences, offers, and new opportunities present themselves seemingly out of nowhere. This can cause you to be unsure about which way to go. It's advisable not to take any wild or frantic actions or be overindulgent. It can be an unpredictable and emotional year that can feel like a rollercoaster with big ups and downs.

The key to navigating this year is to remain still and centred and allow things to come to you as much as possible. Aim to avoid long journeys or moving home. The energy of this year is focused on centring yourself and it can be distracting to make large movements.

It is a year to pause, a time to reassess and analyse. Evaluate the systems you are using in your life from how you do your food shopping to your exercise routine. Are there any tweaks that you can make so that you can fully express yourself? A 5 year is a great time to find yourself and understand your potential. It is a powerful year for growth and healing. A time when you can see connections and how things tie in together, like cause and effect.

New projects that are initiated this year are likely to do very well and have a lasting effect. Along with this you may also find that offers of help and support from unexpected sources arrive and pleasantly surprise you. A great combination for success.

Six Year: Clarity and Focus

Own your power

If your birth number is One:	2018, 2027
If your birth number is Two:	2017, 2026
If your birth number is Three:	2016, 2025
If your birth number is Four:	2015, 2024
If your birth number is Five:	2023, 2032
If your birth number is Six:	2022, 2031
If your birth number is Seven:	2021, 2030
If your birth number is Eight:	2020, 2029
If your birth number is Nine:	2019, 2028

In your 6 year it is typical that you will achieve a new level in your life, perhaps in your career by getting a promotion or retiring or completing a project that is close to your heart. With a growing sense of pride from standing in your power, your skills and talents will be noticed by others. Rewards come to you from the outside world, you'll feel like you have stepped up.

Lead by example, be structured and organised. Let your work express the best of what you can give. This year you have the capacity to focus and get things done, and you will be confident about your endeavours. Reflect on your vision of the future, of your ideal life. Refine your definition of what your ideal life is all about. Ask yourself "Who did I come here to be? What do I want?" This focus enables you to make clear decisions.

Having an authentic purpose helps to raise self-worth and self-esteem. Don't let the anxiety of looking after everyone else stop you from taking care of yourself. Make a conscious effort to tune in and understand the intentions of others whilst focusing on your goals. Communicate in a way that is not overbearing or overly opinionated.

Take time to meditate and breathe. To be able to sit in stillness and quiet takes strength. It's active, not passive. It's a strong, active state. Space clearing or energy clearing are great ways to clear out any stagnant energy to help you connect and gain clarity. Tidying up your space and having a sort-out, are simple ways of doing this.

Seven Year: Reaping Rewards

Joy and Harvest

If your birth number is One:	2019, 2028
If your birth number is Two:	2018, 2027
If your birth number is Three:	2017, 2026
If your birth number is Four:	2016, 2025
If your birth number is Five:	2015, 2024
If your birth number is Six:	2014, 2023
If your birth number is Seven:	2022, 2031
If your birth number is Eight:	2021, 2030
If your birth number is Nine:	2020, 2029

All your efforts over the last few years are now coming together and bearing fruit. It is time for you to receive and celebrate, allow yourself to be open to receiving. It may seem to you like things are coming to you quite effortlessly however this is a direct result of previous effort, find ways to enjoy it.

Take time for celebration, pleasure and self-reward, buy yourself a lovely gift, cook or go out and enjoy beautiful food. Be careful of being too frivolous or taking your good fortune for granted, enjoy it but maintain a good balance. You can treat yourself without upsetting your bank balance.

This can be a very inspirational time for you, a chance to experience beauty such as going out in nature, visiting art galleries or having a good massage. Soak up the preciousness of life by watching butterflies dancing around a Buddleia in full bloom, wear your favourite clothes, use your best tableware and spend time with those you love.

This year reflect on what brings you joy. What brings you pleasure, inspiration and appreciation. Emotionally guard against feelings of sadness due to nostalgia or worry over deprivation, remember our minds can flip to the negative when we appear to be having too much fun! It is right and good to reap what you deserve, perhaps just avoid making careless choices and decisions whilst embracing joy and pleasure.

Eight Year: Deep Change and Transformation

Time to gather

If your birth number is One:	2020, 2029
If your birth number is Two:	2019, 2028
If your birth number is Three:	2018, 2027
If your birth number is Four:	2017, 2026
If your birth number is Five:	2016, 2025
If your birth number is Six:	2015, 2024
If your birth number is Seven:	2023, 2032
If your birth number is Eight:	2022, 2031
If your birth number is Nine:	2021, 2030

The seeds of change are stirring and just like a caterpillar transforming into a butterfly this year may not be comfortable, yet the result is likely to be beautiful. At first it may seem like things just aren't right and this will develop into a deep re-evaluation. This year you will be confronted by all the ways you are not feeling fulfilled. It's OK, you don't have to rush and change everything right now, Eight energy shines a light on the veiled areas, so you are aware and notice. Then you can begin to change in small, measured ways. The change is designed to give you an opportunity to be aligned and happy.

An Eight year is a year of evaluation, to consider what is not working and gather information. Allow quiet time for walks, pondering, study and research. Have plenty of cave time otherwise you are likely to get angry and stomp your feet. Making small changes can help with the frustration, like having your hair cut, getting a tattoo or rearranging the furniture.

Trust the process- it can be a struggle and you may feel resistance as it's difficult to wait and see what's waiting to be born. Attempt to let go. Frustration is a strong motivator, and you may go into 'task mode'; serious and responsible. There can be some communication issues so double check emails, dates and plans. Be mindful to soften any stubbornness, mountains can be moved with love.

9 Fire- Love and Light

In the spotlight

If your birth number is One:	2021, 2030
If your birth number is Two:	2020, 2029
If your birth number is Three:	2019, 2028
If your birth number is Four:	2018, 2027
If your birth number is Five:	2017, 2026
If your birth number is Six:	2016, 2025
If your birth number is Seven:	2015, 2024
If your birth number is Eight:	2023, 2032
If your birth number is Nine:	2022, 2031

Here comes the sun! After the reorientation of the previous year, you are entering a year of full expansion and rapid movement. You'll spend your time either full speed ahead or crash out from exertion. You have a newfound clarity; the clouds have lifted and new ideas and opportunities surface and come to light.

You have now come full circle and all paths become visible. It is a time of completion, some things may come to an end such as projects, jobs or friendships. It is time to put everything into the fire of transformation ready for the next 9-year cycle to begin.

This year is filled with the energy of optimism, clarity, enthusiasm and adventure. A great time for fame and recognition, to get easily noticed. Make use of this time being in the spotlight, it is a good year to powerfully publicise yourself. Have fun, be social and do things that bring you joy.

As the bright light of clarity illuminates everything around you, there is the possibility of some secrets or frailties that you would prefer to remain hidden being brought to light. It is also possible to get overwhelmed by everything that is going on in your hectic year, so slow down now and then to bring projects to a conclusion before following the next shiny object.

17

9 KEY-SELF SOOTHING TOOLS

SELF-SOOTHING ENCAPSULATES ALL THE WAYS THAT YOU CAN COMFORT yourself when thoughts and emotions are overwhelming. Self-soothing is a healing balm that you can give to yourself. Like a warm hug or blanket that wraps around you, holds you close and lets you know that everything is going to be OK. Self-soothing helps you regulate your emotional state and learning how to do it can be an invaluable skill during times of stress and uncertainty.

If you're having a tough time right now, it can feel like there is nothing you can do. I promise you there is. There are so many things you can do to help yourself feel better. Self-soothing is available to you night or day, all you need to do is choose which activity meets your needs in the moment. You may find that you develop a favourite or two and they become your go-to's. Some may seem quite simple, and they are. Sometimes the simplest of things have the most profound results.

When I was at my lowest points, scared, confused and heartbroken using these tools helped me through. They enabled me to fall asleep when I felt alone and ashamed lying in bed in the dark and they gave me strength to face another day by building my confidence and clarity.

Self-soothing activities help you feel safe in your body, regulate your emotions and cope with distressing thoughts and feelings. They activate your parasympathetic nervous system, the soothing state that your body and mind have to rest and digest.

There are many ways to self-soothe including listening to music, sipping a cup of herbal tea like camomile (I like mine with some honey), petting your dog or cat and walking out in nature. I have chosen to highlight below 9 tools that you can use interchangeably with the activities just mentioned, ones that you may not have come across before.

1. Journalling

Journalling or writing your thoughts onto a page is one of the best tools I know to work through and alleviate suffering.

Seeing your thoughts as words reflected back to you is incredibly empowering and insightful. Rather than having the ruminating thoughts swirl around your mind causing havoc, you can observe and catch them. It's like reaching up and catching them in your hand like you would a dandelion seed to make a wish. Any thoughts that no longer serve you can be gently blown away by the breeze as the wind catches them.

Journalling offers you the opportunity to hold your words on the page as they whisper their magical truth to you. Their sparkly glints of wisdom winking at you.

Simply being and sitting with your own thoughts is a gift to yourself. Allowing you the time and space to reflect without the noise and distraction of other energies around you. It has enabled me to hear my own voice, the one that was barely audible before.

Journalling involves a slowing down and an inner honesty. You know your truth, yet sometimes it takes a bit of intention and courage to uncover it. Yes, it's scary and uncomfortable at times, I can hear your reservations. If you sit with the feelings and let them flow through your words, they will dissipate, and you will create more space and peace within you.

Writing down your innermost thoughts does not need to be neat and tidy. There's no requirement for correct spelling and good grammar. Your words can be angry, sad or happy. You can scribble them down hard and fast like there's steam coming off your pen or you can take your time like a meandering walk along a river. The amount of time you spend on it is also up to you, 5 minutes or 3 hours, you're in charge. The key thing is to give it a go and let the wonders of journalling unfold.

If sitting with a blank page feels daunting start with a prompt. Here are a few to get you started.

- ♥ The best things happening in my life now are...
- ♥ I am frustrated, resistant, annoyed about...
- ♥ I feel confused about....
- ♥ I want....

2. Energy Magnet

Your energy can easily be spread out and depleted. What you focus on you give energy to and you may have many 'irons in the fire'. Your energy can fragment and scatter through overthinking and doing things for other people. You know that feeling that everyone wants 'a piece' of you and you don't know whether you are coming or going? That you have several plates spinning and you don't have the energy left for self-care? Your well has dried up because everyone has taken a drink and there's only drops left for you?

Calling your energy back to yourself is a wonderful way to feel whole and peaceful. It helps you to discern if you have any energy leaks. The more energy and resources you have for yourself the less likely you will suffer from frustration or resentment. Commanding tighter boundaries enables you to give your energy mindfully and on your terms.

Call Yourself Home Guided Meditation

To Begin

Allow yourself to settle into a comfortable seated position with your hands resting gently on your lap, palms upwards indicating receiving. Gently close your eyes allowing your attention to go inwards.

Imagine and feel that you are connected to all the love in the Universe and that it is supporting, inspiring and guiding you. To help you connect, turn your lips into a smile and feel the warmth and love radiating through you.

Step 1: Allow all the scattered parts of you to come back

Imagine all of the parts of yourself that have spread out (through being of service to others etc.) all coming back to your centre. Gathering your power back into you like a magnet. You can visualise your centre as a core pillar of light within, like a sparkling tube that runs down from the top of your head to your feet and into the Earth.

Ask that all your scattered particles of energy return to you, call them back.

Breathing in, gathering your power.

See the particles as shimmering points of light being drawn towards your centre

Breathing out, relax into being yourself. Allow yourself to settle knowing that you are gathered.

Step 2: Let go of everything that isn't meant to be in your energy field.

Breathe in and collect any fog, confusion or muck, anything that no longer serves you or is depleting your energy.

On the out breath let it go, send it out. You can imagine it being released into the ground. Mother Earth loves to compost old energies for you.

Take several breaths in and out until you feel clear and present.

Step 3: Fill yourself up

Breathe in and allow yourself to be filled up.

First fill up your core pillar so that it is infused with white light and then see the energy radiate out into every cell in your body infused with love and white light.

Breathe in love and gratitude.

Breathing out and arriving

Let go of the image of your core pillar

Imagine the loving and nurturing energy from Mother Earth filling you up from the soles of your feet to the top of your head. On each in-breath, breathe up the beautiful energy until you feel full and complete.

Allow yourself a few moments here to just be. Nothing to do and nowhere to go.

Allow your breathing to return to its normal rhythm and depth.

When you are ready wiggle your toes and circle your wrists, take a stretch if that feels good. Slowly come back into the room by blinking your eyes open and noticing the space around you.

3. Balance- Rebuild Your Personal Power

If the balance in a relationship has been unequal and there is a power dynamic occurring, the healthiest thing for you to do is rebuild your personal power. To redress the balance and reinstate your sovereignty.

When my husband left, he seemed to have all the control, the power dynamic heavily weighted in his favour which made me feel unsafe, helpless and ashamed.

He left without any proper discussion or explanation. When he moved at first, he would not disclose his address, he refused to share information about his new life, and he withheld money from me. My enquiries were met with cryptic and closed statements like *"I'm safe "*and *"That's none of your business anymore."*

There had been an imbalance in our relationship long before he left, one that was not very apparent to me until I began to see the patterns. I had often kept quiet about my concerns to keep the peace or for fear of being discarded. I had however begun to speak up. To let him know there were some things I didn't agree with, things that felt unfair and that I wanted changes to be made. As it became clear that I would no longer tolerate this imbalance, he voted with his feet.

When there's an imbalance of power, it can show up in many forms, including resentment, endless arguments, and emotional distance. The most common power dynamics in a relationship, where partners attempt to influence each other, are demand/withdrawal, distancer/pursuer, and fear/shame.

Changing the power dynamic in relationships requires trust, vulnerability, and honest and respectful communication. If you have tried these skills without success, then it becomes your choice to empower yourself and decide what is best for you in your life.

How to build your Personal Power

The first step is to acknowledge that you are a human being and that it's OK to see the best in people. Relationships do change and often you are the last person to see the changes because you have faith in the relationship and are invested in it.

Forgive Yourself

When someone close to you surprises you. When you feel that you have been duped. It can make you feel foolish, disappointed and shocked. This is an uncomfortable space to be in. A remedy to move through the discomfort is forgiveness and self-forgiveness.

Whenever a thought or feeling connected with being fooled comes up, choose forgiveness.

Repeat the phrase

Even though I have been misled and I feel foolish, I completely love and accept myself anyway. I forgive myself.

Remember that it's not the snake bite that kills, it is the venom that circulates in the body. Words and actions do have power and can hurt. It is how you continue to process them though that makes the real difference.

Focus on yourself

Rediscover and do all the activities, interests and values that are important to you.

What makes your heart sing? What motivates you? Where would you like to visit?

Do you like the gym, swimming or cycling? Or do you prefer Yoga, Tai Chi or Karate?

Do you enjoy audio books, Kindle or paperback?

What foods do you like? Have you always wanted to learn how to bake like Mary Berry?

Write them all down and make a plan to have a go at least one each week.

Focus on your Positive Traits

Whilst it is important and useful to recognise your weaknesses so you can grow and develop, focusing on your positive traits helps to encourage and motivate you. An exercise to focus on your positive traits is to write down as many of them as you can think of. Then ask trusted friends and family what they see as your positive traits. Aim for 25 traits on your list. Whenever you are feeling low, look at the list to remind yourself how wonderful you are.

4. Ho'oponopono

Ho'oponopono is a Hawaiian forgiveness ritual that you can use if something is troubling you. If you are upset or suffering and it doesn't seem to be going away, if you feel betrayed or hurt and cannot shake it off, it is a wonderful method of healing.

Method

Focus on the person or problem and then repeat these words as a mantra as many times as you need to until you feel a shift. You may like to put one hand on your heart and one on your tummy or both hands on your heart whilst practicing Ho'oponopono.

Whilst practicing this mantra, tears may flow and a felt sense that your body and mind is relaxing, will develop. The experience can be beautifully uplifting as you let go of heavy negative thoughts and energy and allow the space to be filled with love and gratitude.

Mantra

I am sorry

Please forgive me

I love you

Thank you

The practice of Ho'oponopono is based on taking self-responsibility for anything that affects your state of being and is a simple and powerful method of healing. Ho'o means cause whilst "ponopono" means perfection and roughly translates to 'make things move back into balance'. The practice teaches the importance of love and forgiveness through a process that allows you to relinquish your burdens so that you can heal.

Forgiveness is a skill that aids your recovery from the anger and distress of negative experiences. Saying these words helps you to navigate through tricky emotions. Practicing Ho'oponopono is an act of personal strength and courage where you can approach your future with a clean slate. It encourages and distils within you an openness to interactions without blame, shame or resentment.

Ho'oponopono encourages you to recognise that your core motivations, the energy you put out, affect what you attract towards you. Practicing the art of forgiveness and acceptance cleanses your heart and mind so that you can find contentment.

5. Embrace Vulnerability

Vulnerability is the willingness to be open, to show your emotions and share your insecurities. Being vulnerable can be very challenging. It can feel unsafe, exposing and even shameful when something has changed in your life that you weren't prepared for. Vulnerability has been portrayed as a negative thing by past generations and in the UK the idea of the stiff upper lip has immortalised it. Therefore, you have likely grown up with the messages that being vulnerable is wrong or not appropriate.

Whilst you may face barriers to embracing vulnerability such as previously being rejected, feeling uncomfortable about sharing your emotions or crying in front of someone, it's a beautiful gift to share your genuine thoughts and feelings. If you cope with life's challenges by bottling it all up, you may be festering resentment, expressing emotions in unhealthy ways or be in a relationship that is toxic for you.

Vulnerability can provide a sense of belonging which is essential to your well-being. If you learn your barriers to openness, you can take steps to overcome them and enjoy a better sense of connection with others. Speaking from your heart and sharing details about you and your life allows the listener to understand you at a deeper level. To get a real sense of you. Embracing vulnerability helps the people around you do the same and can cultivate intimacy and trust in your relationships.

Embracing vulnerability did not come easy to me. I resisted it because it felt too scary, and partly because it wasn't welcomed or supported in my marriage. We are often taught as children to be 'nice', to be 'good' and 'not to rock the boat'. We then translate that message into people who will only like or love us if we are 'good.' That is what I believed.

The question "What about me?" started to pop into my mind quite often. I noticed that I was consistently being put on the bottom of the priority list, left on the sidelines unless it had been deemed, I had done or achieved something 'good'. I was questioned daily about what I had been 'up to', naively I considered this as interest until it became painfully clear that it was in fact something much more unpleasant.

I could feel the contrast between interest and disappointment radiating out from him. On the days when I mentioned I had created income for the household, there was interest and praise. On the days I had excitedly listed what I had done for me or to build on my business there was an air of displeasure. I remember the squirmy sensation at the pit of my stomach when he asked what jobs had been done around the house or what was for dinner rather than celebrating my personal growth with me. At first, I considered the thought, "What about me? "a little childish, like I was whining or being selfish. Then I realised that it was much bigger and deeper than that.

Once I truly understood the gravity of what I was asking of myself and how deeply answering this question would affect my life, I began to tentatively ask trusted friends for their views and guidance. I was met with validation, concern and humour! Once the question gained momentum in my system, my self-worth had been activated, going from being quite dormant to turned up to full. When I began to lightly question him about my concerns and what we could do about them, it wasn't too long before he chose to discard me.

What about me? Is a question that is generally posed when you are feeling very depleted, when you've reached the last straw. It can be something so small that triggers it and yet underneath this question is a sea of unmet needs. Your needs can only truly be met by you, yourself. However, it's important to be brave and communicate them to others as well.

It's better to know the truth than to live a lie. To know who welcomes your authenticity and honesty and who does not value it. Vulnerability received and held in a loving, caring way is a beautiful gift to bestow on someone. Vulnerability in the hands of someone who has earned your trust, who sees your inner and outer beauty, melts away any misgivings. Vulnerability is worth the effort. I'm so glad I can now use it as one of my superpowers.

6. Unconditional Love Exercise

Metta Loving Kindness Meditation

When you are going through something difficult, your fear or contraction can make you feel alone. Practicing compassion and in particular Loving-Kindness helps you to be a better friend to yourself. To adopt a gentler attitude towards yourself and create a feeling of calm and safety. Practicing this meditation can help you to let yourself 'off the hook' more often and bring some kindness towards yourself on both good and bad days.

During Loving Kindness Meditation, you focus benevolent and loving energy toward yourself and others. It's a practice that reminds you that every living being, including yourself wishes to live in peace and happiness.

The phrases need to be meaningful to you, heartfelt and profound, that you would wish for yourself and wish for others. Here are some commonly used phrases that you can begin with, feel free to adapt them.

May I be peaceful

May I be safe

May I be happy

May I live with ease

May I be free from suffering

Sometimes, perhaps often, offering these phrases will seem very ordinary, dry or mechanical, but that's OK. It doesn't mean that nothing is happening or that it's not working. What's important is to do it, to practice saying the phrases. Form an intention to use them to relieve suffering. You are uniting the power of loving-kindness and the power of intention and that is what will produce the effect of free-flowing loving-kindness.

Guided Loving Kindness Meditation

To begin, sit in a comfortable position with your back upright. Close your eyes and bring your attention to your breath.

Find the phrases you would like to use to offer good wishes. Take a few deep breaths, relaxing the body. Repeat very gently the phrases that reflect what you wish most deeply for yourself. For example:

May I be peaceful

May I be healthy

May I be happy

May I live with ease

May I know love

It may help you to connect to the loving essence of the phrases by placing a hand or two hands on your heart as you bring them to mind.

Take a moment to truly feel and comprehend the meaning of each phrase. You can repeat a phrase more than once or you may choose a single word and repeat this to yourself. The main beauty of this practice is in the intention.

If you notice that your mind starts to wander, simply return your attention to these phrases. Remember it's normal to get distracted.

Before you complete your practice, you may like to offer the following phrases:

May I and all other beings be peaceful

May I and all other beings be healthy

May I and all other beings be happy

May I and all other beings know love

7. Grounding

Grounding is a practice of energetically connecting to the Earth's natural electric charge that steadies and heals you at the deepest levels. Practicing grounding reduces stress and generates greater well-being. Grounding is an effective way to calm anxiety.

It brings you back into your body instead of living up in your head, which may be swirling. It is a lovely way to self-soothe as it is relaxing and comforting to feel 'in your body'. It gives you a sense of security and safety, that you have all your wits and senses available to you. Being grounded means that you are confident and sure of yourself.

When you're grounded, you have a strong connection with who you are. You're in control of your mental and emotional self, and not easily influenced by other ideas or individuals. You allow life's small mishaps to roll off your shoulders. For example, if someone cuts you off in traffic, you may give a shoulder shrug, and think, "Oh, well, they must be in a hurry." You won't become overwhelmed by, or reactive to, the incident.

Grounding- connecting to the Earth

Grounding at its root is the practice of connecting to the Earth to soothe and heal you. You can imagine its effects like a plant growing from a stable and nourishing plot of land. It will stand taller and grow stronger if it is supported and nurtured by an unconditionally loving source. Simply taking your shoes and socks off and standing on the Earth and taking some deep breaths is relaxing and nourishing. You can lie down on the Earth and feel the healing support, or you can use grounding techniques.

I find grounding extremely useful. When I was suffering the most in the early days and months after my breakup, I would often go outside, day or night, whether it was warm or cold, whip my socks off and stand on the grass. I could feel the tension, pain and grief draining from me into the ground as I took some deep breaths and let go. Sometimes I would include shaking my arms and hands to release any stubborn pent-up energy. After standing for a few minutes or sometimes longer I always feel more self-assured, contented and calm.

8. Let Go

Letting go of someone or something for most of us is not an easy thing to do. Letting go can be scary as it is stepping into the unknown. You may imagine or have thoughts of something ending up much worse than before. Or that you may lose the thing forever. For example, you may think that you will never have the same depth of love, the quality of friendship or the camaraderie as you had with this relationship, friendship or job.

If thoughts like this arise, I invite you to consider the phrases *'As one door closes another one open's'* and *'What's for you, won't pass you by.'*

Of course, each relationship and situation are different, however this is not a negative thing. Each time you meet new people and have a variety of experiences, your world expands. Exposing yourself to novel people, activities and perceptions, enables you to see through a new lens, creating opportunities for enhanced fun, fulfilment and personal growth.

Letting go and allowing what will be to unfold involves trust. If you have been betrayed or disappointed in the past, then rebuilding trust may be required. Making a conscious decision to let go of the past- to forgive yourself and others can help to achieve this. Holding onto old negative memories takes up space, space that you could free up to enable fresh energy to blow into your life.

Leave exaggerated or negative thoughts behind, put down any worries or concerns and bring in gratitude for yourself and all the good things in your life. Let the love in that is all around you. This creates space for new opportunities for growth and manifestation.

Here's a useful reminder in the form of the acronym, LET GO

L- leave

E- exaggerated or negative

T- thoughts

G- gratitude

O- opportunities

9. Find a Lighter Thought Tool

It had snowed in Northumberland overnight, a good sprinkling of that lovely light fluffy snow that's really white. The glorious bright sunshine we woke up to made the snow glisten and sparkle.

As I was feeling uplifted, when Iris and I got into the car, I thought it would be fun to play with the snow a little. I opened the windows and watched as the snow that had been collected on the glass remained intact and stood to attention, suspended in mid-air for a moment. On closer inspection as the light streamed through the snow, the individual snowflakes came into focus with their beautiful intricate patterns, they were a lovely sight.

Then some of the snow folded in on itself and fell inside the car, I laughed enjoying the moment. A little while before that however was a different story, a different mood. I had noticed myself getting caught up in some 'heavy' thoughts. Thoughts of worry and concern about the future. I felt gravity was taking my chin closer to the floor and my head becoming like lead on my shoulders. As soon as I recognised what my body was doing, I immediately caught my train of thought.

As I am luckily well practiced in catching my thoughts, the moment I recognised I was beginning to be carried away by them, that they were about to spiral negatively perhaps out of control, the sentence *Find a lighter thought* popped into my awareness. It made me smile, I gave myself a self-compassionate inner hug and reached for a more positive dialogue. For a higher vibration.

My body straightened, my head lifted, my shoulders went back and down, and I felt happy once again.

Find a Lighter Thought Tool

Take a moment to tune into your body and notice how it feels. Once you recognise there is a level of discomfort, take your mind back to what you were thinking. Notice any heavy kind of thoughts and find a lighter thought instead. Reframe the negative into more of a positive, in other words think the opposite. It may take a few attempts to reach a lighter thought. Once you do find a lighter thought, tune in again to your body and you will likely notice that your whole being feels lighter.

Example:

Heavy thought train

I've got so much to do, how am I going to fit it all in. I think I'm starting to get a cold; I hope it's not going to be too busy at work later.

Lighter thought train

There's plenty of time to do everything I want to do. It's the weekend tomorrow. I really enjoy my work and the people are wonderful.

Lighter thoughts are encouraging, motivating and put you back to *feeling* in control. Negative and heavy thoughts are not very productive and can drag you down. If you are dragged down far enough you can start to believe that you have no control, no safety which can lead to stress and depression. Give yourself the gift of a lighter thought, come on, let's jump on that train choo choo!!

Part 5
PATHS TO CLARITY

18

ROLE MODELS

A YOUNG BOY WAS HAPPILY PLAYING IN HIS GARDEN ON A BRIGHT sunny day. He squealed with glee as he ran rings around his brother playing tag. They climbed their favourite tree as they had done many times before. Then there was a snap and a crack and a big thud. The branch had snapped, and the boy fell from the tree cutting his knee.

His mother, upon hearing the commotion came outside and soothed him. She showed him compassion and concern. Gave him a cuddle, put a plaster on his knee and let him know he was OK.

The following week, the boy is playing football with his friend on the school field and his friend goes for a tackle and hurts his leg. He drops to the ground gripping his leg and shouting in pain.

The boy runs over to his friend and shows him kindness. He helps him up and then supports him as he hops off the field.

Sometime later, the boy fails his maths test. He had tried his best and yet there were questions he just didn't know the answer to. Alone in his bedroom and feeling a bit sad about having to retake the test, he is compassionate towards himself. He offers soothing words of encouragement to himself.

He has learnt to internalise his role models' positive and nurturing responses and so was then able to model that behaviour to his friend and to himself. Unfortunately, this is not always the case. Not everyone grows up learning or having modelled to them care and compassion.

For example, when my husband left the Matriarch closed ranks, not only did my children lose their dad, but they also essentially lost the whole side of his family. Birthday cards and Christmas wishes stopped. A complete shutout, seemingly encouraged by a grandmother. My heart broke into more pieces not so much for me but for my children.

It made sense to me then why my husband behaved in the ways he did. Stonewalling, withholding, blaming and controlling were just some of the ways he conducted himself because that was all he knew to do.

As much as I attempted to show him a different way, his patterns were ingrained. I eventually realised that as much as I loved him it was a fruitless task attempting to alter his perceptions, his mind was made up. Whilst he had a choice to join me on a journey of personal growth, it was absolutely his right not to take up my invitation.

> *"The more you love someone, the more you touch their pain."*
> -Jeffrey Allen.

In a relationship, you both bring to the surface the hurts that are underlying and available to heal. You each bring out these pains and wounds so that they can be recognised and explored. It's one of the beautiful gifts of being in a relationship, the chance to gently and compassionately show your loved one where their hurts are and give them the opportunity to work on them. It's your job to be kind and it's their job to choose whether they are willing to heal or not.

I discovered that the more I found love for myself, and asked for what I wanted and needed the quicker our relationship changed. The enhanced quality and depth of my love began to transform me and then radiated outwards. It was felt. It touched him. It was then a matter of choice for us as individuals what to do with this new level of awareness.

It intrigued me how these patterns came to be. I wanted to find out more, to understand, heal and learn so that I could be the best role model I could be for our children. Rather than getting bogged down in blame, judgement or feeling like a victim, I took the stance of the 'beginner's mind'.

I remembered that I had learnt about Attachment Styles a few years before and they piqued my interest again. They offer a model of how we learn to be in relationships, and I was hopeful they would offer me some clarity. I immersed myself in the topic, pulled out my books on the subject and attended a few online courses. I had many light bulb moments.

19

ATTACHMENT STYLES- THE DANCE OF CONNECTION

LOVE AND CONNECTION ARE EXTRAORDINARILY IMPORTANT FOR human beings- you are hardwired for connection.

The dance of connection happens whenever you interact with others. The moment you are interacting with someone, their rules on how to relate with others will dance with yours. There is probably nothing that impacts you more than your attachment style when it comes to relationships.

Connection with others changes the way you see yourself, and how you perceive others, and it changes the way you view the world. Connection changes your physical well-being and impacts your level of life satisfaction and how much you love yourself. Your attachment style rules also have a major impact on how you feel about romantic relationships in general. They impact the way you feel about commitment, closeness, connection and communication.

Knowing how to be in relationships is not automatic. Most likely you have not been taught directly what to look for in a secure partnership. That's OK. Bringing awareness to it now means that you will be more discerning about your patterns and those of your loved ones in future.

Your attachment style is essentially the set of rules you are subconsciously wired to play by when it comes to connecting with others, as a result of your childhood experiences of attachment and connection to your caregivers.

Like any other skill, being in a healthy, balanced and loving relationship takes knowledge and practice. Relationships can be very difficult when you have different attachment styles from the people you love, because you are playing the game of connection differently. Awareness of attachment styles can open a whole new way for you to approach relationships, starting with the most important one, the one you have with yourself.

There are 3 Main Attachment Styles

Secure

Avoidant

Anxious

Secure Attachment is characterised by self-worth, self-reliance, emotional maturity, and honest communication.

Securely attached people enjoy intimacy and are comfortable with it. They are emotionally intelligent- understand emotions and show empathy. They hold the belief that the world is safe and predictable. They tend to provide emotional and practical support, without withdrawing or playing any games. They give, but they also expect to get back.

Avoidant Attachment is characterised by someone avoiding vulnerability, closeness, and intimate attachment to others.

An avoidantly attached person may avoid relationships and crave independence, they don't value close relationships like the other styles do. They may be very social, easy-going, fun to be around and yet are happy to be alone. They tend to be steady, reliable, good problem solvers who get the job done.

Anxious Attachment is characterised by someone who is anxious in relationships and has low self-esteem.

They want to be close to others but are afraid that people don't want to be with them. They are very attuned to their partner's needs and sensitive to the relationship's needs.

Anxiously attached people tend to give a great amount and settle a lot to make relationships work. When they feel the relationship is threatened, they will attempt to control the situation.

An important note to remember is that attachment styles are not personal. They are learnt. The good news is, you can relearn and move towards a secure attachment style.

In the rest of this chapter, I am going look at these 3 attachment styles in depth and there are going to be some exercises that can help you to determine your attachment style.

Take 5 Pause and Practice

Give yourself a point for each question or statement below that you say yes to:

- ♥ Do you ignore problems or pretend they are not happening?
- ♥ Do you believe that circumstances aren't that bad?
- ♥ Do you avoid asking for what you want and need?
- ♥ Do you stay in relationships where you have been betrayed? Where they have been untrustworthy? Where they have been rude to you? Disrespectful or cruel?
- ♥ Are you afraid of making mistakes or struggle to make decisions?

- ♥ Do you think deep down that you are not worthy enough, lovable enough?
- ♥ Do you end relationships too soon because you have an urge to be independent?
- ♥ I seek out approval or the thoughts of others rather than trusting myself
- ♥ I feel compelled to help people solve their problems
- ♥ I anticipate other people's needs and wonder why they don't do the same for me.

Did you say yes to all these questions? Or perhaps a few in particular?

If your points totalled:

1-3   You are generally self-aware and have a good sense of self-worth
4-6   There are times when your patterns are causing unhealthy behaviours
7-10 You're in the right place to start putting yourself at the centre of your Universe

The higher your score the more likely it is that you would benefit from learning how to love and connect with yourself more. To move towards being securely attached and understanding what true love and intimacy can offer. Putting yourself first and remembering that you are the most important person in your world.

Ops I Forgot About Me

I was having dinner with my lovely Mum, one night and we were talking about how many 'beings' I have in my care, and I remarked that I have 6. Alfie, Iris, Maya and Pepper our dogs and Maisie and Merlin our cats.

Mum looked at me with a quizzical look and said no there's 7. I counted again and then realised what she was saying. The 7th person is me! I completely discounted myself.

This realisation stopped me in my tracks and caused me to ponder. I was quite shocked and taken aback that I had not thought about myself. I felt a heaviness in my chest and a wave of despondence wash over me. How could I have forgotten about myself? The thought disturbed me. I said it out loud as a response to my exasperation *"How did I forget about myself?"*

I consider myself as a person who likes herself, who is emotionally intelligent and thoughtful and yet I did not factor myself into the equation. This loving comment from my Mum made me (figuratively) stand up and want to make a change. It encouraged me to remember that I am important and that I deserve to be nourished too.

It is an oversight that I'm sure mums, dads and partners the world over will recognise.

Remember please to take care of yourself, first and foremost. Think of filling your cup up first so that you can then nurture all the beings in your care from the overflow, rather than parching yourself. You don't want to turn into a dried-up husk!

Ingredients of a Good Relationship

When I began to delve into the world of attachment styles, what really stood out to me was the ingredients needed to feel good about myself and others whilst in a relationship. The more I learnt about the different styles the more parallels I could identify within myself and what had been out of balance in my marriage.

The checklists and tips for how to be securely attached gave me something to aim for. A guideline for where my growth areas were. This reassured me as I was concerned, as you may be, that I would fall into the same patterns again. I wanted to take the time to heal and develop as an individual before testing out my new way of being with someone new.

A reminder- it's when you are in a relationship with others that your patterns will emerge. That's where the learning and magic happen.

The Goal of Secure Attachment

I feel good about myself, and I feel good about other people.

Here's a checklist that you can mentally or physically tick off to let you know the areas where you are securely attached. It also serves as a guideline for personal growth areas.

Being securely attached does not mean that you are always confident. There may be some occasions when you have difficulty identifying or communicating your emotions. Or times when you aren't assertive or speak directly. Overall, however, you will be able to form healthy relationships, be comfortable on your own and have the ability to manage your emotions.

Secure Attachment Checklist

- ♥ You can connect with yourself and others
- ♥ You can communicate well
- ♥ You have healthy boundaries
- ♥ You are OK in alone time
- ♥ You feel fundamentally safe
- ♥ You trust relationships
- ♥ You have appropriate and healthy boundaries
- ♥ You have a good self-esteem
- ♥ You do not shame yourself or others
- ♥ You have fulfilling and meaningful relationships
- ♥ You can be vulnerable and open in love

I hope this checklist provides you with some insights and food for thought.

I invite you to journal on what you have learnt from these statements and how they made you feel.

The Tortoise and The Bull

There are two very typical attachment styles many people fall into, either in family dynamics or in close romantic relationships. They are the avoidant and anxious attachment styles.

When you love someone there is a general expectation that they will behave in kind and loving ways towards you no matter what. You may be accustomed to their thoughtful gestures, bids for connection and warm reassuring hugs.

It is then a confusing, painful shock to the system when during a time of upset or stress such as the threat of divorce or the loss of a job, where they behave in ways that are alien to you. At a time, perhaps when you would benefit the most from support and compassion, on the face of it, they are unavailable to you.

Times of stress and trauma can bring out learnt coping mechanisms. When faced with these experiences you are likely to display an aspect of one out of two different strategies, either to withdraw or confront. In many relationships one partner will be the 'tortoise' and the other a 'bull'.

This dynamic can help both people to recognise their patterns and to seek to heal them. To dance towards secure attachment. Unfortunately, as relationships, like babies don't come with manuals, attachment styles and their effect on relationships are not widely known and so many of us don't recognise the dance or the steps.

The Tortoise

If you are the tortoise, when triggered, your coping response will be to go into your shell, hide and withdraw. You may say things that dismiss other people's feelings, brush them off and invalidate them.

Saying things like:

"What's the big deal?"

"I'm sorry you feel that way."

"You shouldn't feel that way."

"Don't think about it, just get on with it."

"I'm not having this discussion!"

These kinds of words and actions are very painful for the 'Bull' in particular.

Attempting to hide from the pain, not wanting to feel it, causes unnecessary anguish to you and those close to you. Hiding from the pain and stuffing it down is a temporary fix. Those emotions are stored in your body and if not let out, felt and healed they will come out in bursts of frustration and anger at unpredictable times.

When you attempt not to feel pain, you also cheat yourself out of feeling love and joy.

> *"We cannot selectively numb emotions, when we numb the painful emotions, we also numb the positive emotions."*
> -Brene Brown

The Bull

If you are a bull, your coping mechanism when triggered is to confront, to chase validation. You may say things in an attempt to have your emotions respected or to test someone's reaction.

Things you may say or do:

"I want to discuss this right now".

Exaggerate to gain sympathy

Overreact and go on the attack

Slam doors and shout

Bring up past hurt not relating to the issue

These kinds of words and behaviour can feel very confrontational to a tortoise. The result of this is that the tortoise will retreat more, and the bull will charge towards them more.

The Bull in you is essentially frightened and anxious and so you attempt to confront as a coping mechanism. To seem strong and in control. You don't want to feel vulnerable or anxious.

Healthy ways to reduce the 'charge' and drama are to find ways to meet your own needs, to self-soothe and to accept that vulnerability is a superpower. Being aware of which strategy you adopt i.e.; tortoise or bull can help you to move away from painful ways of coping in difficult situations and towards more helpful ways of self-regulation and self-soothing.

Let me now take you deeper into the characteristics of the Tortoise and The Bull. Understanding where these behaviours, thoughts and feelings came from can be validating and an aid to healing and growth.

Avoidant Attachment Style

The Emotionally Unavailable Person- also known as The Tortoise

This attachment style occurs when there has been prolonged emotional neglect. This neglect can sometimes be overlooked because the child's physical and intellectual needs are met, whilst the emotional needs are not. It's very common for the avoidant to be unaware that something is missing because they perceive themselves to have had a good childhood.

Some of the core wounds of the avoidant include: "I am defective, I am bad, I am unsafe, I am trapped"

A person with an avoidant attachment is usually a gentle person who is fearful of connection and confused about love. They didn't have anyone to mirror their emotions, or how they were feeling inside, to understand and hear them and so they had to rely on themselves. This over-focus on themselves is a reaction to earlier disappointments at being let down.

They expect to be hurt or that no one will be there for them when they reach out for connection.

The avoidant often fears being smothered or invaded in romantic relationships. This makes them feel trapped and powerless. In their perception if they give too much or get too close that their resources will be stolen or taken away. Including sharing aspects of themselves.

This leads to using a survival strategy of tending to take more than they give, they are focused on hoarding what they have to stay afloat, to stay alive. They have a high need for security, their home is likely to be a sanctuary or safe haven.

Please remember that this is not personal, it's a symptom of their nervous system being in flight or fight mode. It is happening often outside of conscious awareness or choice, until it is intentionally brought to the surface to be explored and healed.

Abandonment/ Dismissive

Abandonment is a fear of the avoidant.

They assume that they will be abandoned at some point and so they build positive associations to being alone. They keep their space and distance as alone time gives them a sense of relief. They have a pattern of dismissing other people's feelings, thoughts or ideas as another way of maintaining a level of disconnection, so they avoid the pain of being hurt.

Anxiety

When there is a lot of fear-based thinking happening, it affects the nervous system. Thoughts like *"I am not good enough"*, *"Something is wrong with me"* and a sensitivity to criticism can mean that a person can spend a lot of time in fight, flight, freeze mode. With a background feeling of nervousness or anxiety, they have a hard time sitting still. Choosing to immerse themselves in doing something and losing themselves in it, inadvertently reinforces abandoning their emotional self.

Emotions

Emotions are seen as bad or feared to be unsafe. Vulnerability is viewed as unsafe. They believe that conflict is bad and that it can signal the end of a relationship when in fact it is a healthy part of a relationship. In conflict they will try and escape, deflect and run away. Emotions are feared because they have not learnt how to access and regulate them. Therefore, the use of disagreements to make space, or to 'clear the air' is frightening.

Decisions

People with an avoidant pattern can be indecisive. All decisions are emotionally based so making decisions can be hard because they find it tough to access emotions.

When you are disconnected from your emotions it can be hard to be clear about your decisions. Your emotions are a guiding light and when that light is dimmed it can be difficult to see where to go.

Later in life, especially during times of change or when an important decision needs to be made, they become attached to their parent's approval. This is due to having a small amount of emotional connection with them which is amplified. They can care very deeply about what their parents think and will make decisions to make them happy.

They can feel unheard and misunderstood because they are absorbing other people's emotions and not hearing or connecting with theirs. It takes quite some time for them to be able to process their emotions and to speak up for what they want and need.

Flaws

Avoidant people in a romantic relationship tend to focus on their partner's flaws. Noticing little details and using them as justifications for nitpicking and keeping partners at arm's length or pushing them away. This helps them to feel safe by not allowing themselves to get too close as they believe that truly committing and being vulnerable is not safe.

Rather than attempting to solve the issues in the relationship, finding faults and flaws feels more comfortable. Especially with the underlying beliefs of 'this will never work anyway', 'this person is too emotional', 'this is going to end', or 'the person will leave anyway so I should just push them away now'.

The avoidant's lesson is to learn how to be dependent without feeling overly vulnerable.

Anxious Attachment Style- The Bull

This attachment style tends to come from a childhood where the parents were on then off, very inconsistent with their time and balance of emotions. Leaving the child trying to figure out when they could connect and when they could not connect to the parent. Parents may have been very busy and focused elsewhere, unavailable or unaware of the child's present needs. As well as being either emotionally volatile, shouting and or emotionally passive and easy-going, therefore not offering a sense of grounding or stability.

In a relationship they can feel like the other person is a moving target, never quite sure when they can connect.

The child then starts to think *"Is it me?"*, *"Am I not lovable enough?"*

These beliefs feed a lack of self-esteem and put a lot of energy into proving themselves worthy of love and attention. They can put a lot of effort into proving themselves to be the 'right person'.

Attuning to the needs of the partner or other person, instead of or before their own needs becomes the norm which can be exhausting. Being outwardly focused rather than inwardly focused means a lack of attention paid to themselves. Emotional bankruptcy and even resentment can build due to being unable to articulate their own needs.

People with a pattern towards fear and anxiety respond to their confusion around connection by being hyper-alert to any cues. These cues can be misconstrued and be interpreted negatively, leading to deep hurt.

People with an anxious tendency need to find ways to self-soothe and self-regulate.

Complaining

Sometimes the anxious person will attempt to get their needs met by complaining. Their bids for support may sound demanding or attacking which can be off-putting to the person on the receiving end.

Complaining is likely to be a last resort for the anxious person who has attempted to express their needs without being appropriately answered. They may have asked for what they wanted or needed in a way they hoped would get them the response they required and yet it did not. Therefore, if the requirement is still present the anxious person will up the ante to complaining.

They aren't choosing to be negative, it's part of what has been wired into their nervous system, like a 'signal cry' from a baby. Babies cry to express their needs and emotions, when they have had enough of something they will have a fussy, whiny cry.

Old Wounds

It is hard for them to heal old wounds and they tend to hold onto hurts for a long time. They dredge up old stuff when they are triggered and say things like:

"You did this thing in 1977" and then use this as a starting point to bring up everything else that they are unhappy about.

The anxious person's lesson is to learn how to be more independent. The more you do for yourself, the more choice, stability and support.

"Love holds no records of wrongs" is a powerful statement to consider when learning to heal this attachment style.

Rejection

Anxiously attached people enjoy connection and meaningful relationships and therefore fear rejection. They tend to dislike being out of a relationship and so will go to great lengths to hold onto or remain in a relationship. They may offer the other person time and space to consider things carefully. They might suggest counselling or other forms of reconnection like more date nights.

An anxiously attached person may feel that they are not adequate or lovable enough for another relationship. They may cling to one that is not healthy for them fearing that no other relationship will be as good.

Approval

The anxiously attached person can put other people on pedestals, believing that other people are better or more superior to them. This can lead to people pleasing and putting their needs aside to win the approval of others.

This is a survival strategy and comes from the times we were hunter-gatherers- the Neanderthals. In those times if you were ostracised or cast out of the community for some reason you would not survive- the conditions were too harsh. It was much safer to be part of a tribe. Therefore, because you still have the ancient part of your brain- the limbic brain you equate approval with survival.

Take 5 Pause and Practice

Now that you have a flavour of the secure, avoidant and anxious attachment styles, I invite you to look at the questions below with a new lens.

Do any of the questions jump out at you? Perhaps give you a jolt?

If so, I invite you to get quiet and comfortable. To listen to your thoughts and tune into your feelings and journal on your discoveries.

Questions to ask yourself

- ♥ Is/ Was this relationship for you?
- ♥ Are your boundaries honoured and respected?
- ♥ Do you trust yourself or do you question yourself in this relationship?
- ♥ Are your needs being met in the relationship?
- ♥ When you express your needs are you shamed? Or do they do their best to accommodate them?
- ♥ Are they able to ask for their needs to be met? Can you meet them?
- ♥ Is the relationship safe? Are they protective (not overly)?
- ♥ Are they interested, connected and engaged in what you say and do?

Love allows, honours, and appreciates; attachment grasps, demands, needs, and aims to possess.

You've changed

A phrase that you are likely to hear from someone who doesn't like the positive, more empowered and assertive changes in you. If you hear this phrase, I encourage you to celebrate not commiserate.

It may sound like, *"You used to be so sweet and caring, what happened?"* *"You've changed and are cold or closed."*

One Sunday morning, I was having a conversation with my friend John. We both like Tarot cards and often check in with each other to ask what we feel the card reading is advising us. Sharing ideas can help offer new insights that we hadn't noticed before.

John asked me, *"If you were a Tarot card which one would you be?"* He then suggested that he sees a lot of the qualities of the Queen of Swords in me. At first this made me bristle slightly which caught me by surprise. I reflected on this and realised that I had recently been accused of being cold for standing in my power and maintaining my boundaries.

Being cold is not a quality that I want to be associated with, quite the opposite. It felt like a harsh putdown at first from my soon-to-be ex-husband. I was aware, thankfully that being called 'cold' was a tactic to shame me into acquiescing. Once I put the two together, I was pleased with my growth- that standing in my power was being recognised albeit being resisted. I was then able to refocus on the spirit of John's suggestion in the friendly way he meant it.

John showed me a beautifully illustrated Queen of Swords card from one of his card deck collections. She was depicted as wise, strong and kind. Holding a beautiful Owl, with a gentle, etheric, atmospheric tone. This piqued my interest. I asked him if I could see all the variations of cards within his collection that depict the Queen of Swords.

He sent several to me and seeing the range of images laid out, a pattern quickly emerged in my mind. The traditional decks show a Queen holding a sword upright in one hand, whilst sitting on a stone throne. Common interpretations are that she is intelligent, independent and yet cold or hard-natured. Has high standards and is very critical of herself and others.

I knew that John did not see me as a cold-hearted or critical person. What he does recognise is my strength. That I can (now) hold healthy boundaries, be assertive and be very nurturing and supportive. That I have sovereignty over my life and emotions.

The range of images that modern cards now depict the Queen of Swords has caught up with how intelligent, creative and self-reliant women are. They show the positive change in society's trend towards depicting women as powerful and nurturing. Whilst traditionalists would have strong women portrayed as cold and heartless. The modern take is that we are strong, have a voice and know what to do to make our ideas a reality.

If you have been branded as cold or aloof when freeing yourself from the disempowered version of you by the person or persons that would have you stay small, consider it a triumph. Give yourself full permission to move forward boldly, with your head held high.

Take 5 Pause and Practice

The suit of Swords or Air in Tarot is that of the intellect. An opportunity to look at things logically. To cut free what no longer serves you.

Take a moment to consider what would serve you to cut free, to let go.

It could be habits, thoughts, clutter or even friendships or relationships.

Take time to determine if there are any loose ends that you are resistant to letting go of so that you may address them and deal with them straight away.

This is not an exercise of the heart; this is an exercise of the head.

Take out your journal and pen and take an inventory for yourself. Look at your patterns and what may still be hiding and shine a light on them. This is a time to be fully in your power.

20

NINE STAR KI MANDALA REFLECTION EXERCISE

WHEN EXPERIENCING THE TRAUMA OF AND SHOCK OF UNEXPECTED change, grief or loss we can feel overwhelmed, confused and alone.

During these tumultuous times I have found that having a map or a set of guidelines to follow is helpful and comforting. Rather than that disconcerting feeling you are walking down a dark tunnel unable to see what is around you and in front of you. Having a guide turns the light on that leads the way. It's like having an invisible, yet loving force moving you forward whilst holding your hand and whispering in your ear *"All is well."*

Knowing that you are not alone, and that help is always at hand in a myriad of ways offers peace and reassurance. Being aware of your inner resources is also invaluable. When you can tap into your own source of peace, love and happiness it allows you to look out at the world around you from a place of stable calm and enables you to simply notice rather than getting swept up in it all.

You can imagine this as you are the anchor of your ship. When your anchor is employed in rough seas it allows you to remain steadfast. To take it a little further, it is your job to become aware of what situations inside the ship, as well as the conditions at sea cause mighty crashing waves and small ripples in your emotions. Having that level of awareness gives you autonomy in your life.

Connecting with your Nine Star Ki helps to deepen your appreciation for who you are and the transformations you go through in life. It's a tool that facilitates openness, connection and reflection.

The Nine Star Ki Mandala can be used as an energy map- a compass that indicates life areas to be balanced. It offers a systematic way of tapping into and evaluating how balanced your life is and ways to enhance it.

Through the 9-year and 9-month cycles of the system you can track what you have learnt and how much more balanced you are over time. The cycles behave like a spiral. Whilst the energies follow the same predictable pattern, each cycle and your journey through them will naturally involve different experiences that you can then compare.

Connecting to each of the Nine energies and experiencing the essence of them gives you a depth of embodied knowledge that is not possible by simply reading or thinking about them. Just like the difference between listening to a great song on the radio and going to see the singer in concert. Experiencing the singer in concert is a treat for all the senses, you can fully immerse yourself in the atmosphere and it leaves you feeling upbeat and relaxed.

Directions

Nine Star Ki Mandala

Allow yourself some space and time with no distractions. Sit comfortably with your feet placed on the floor and your hands resting gently on your lap. Take a few deep relaxing breaths right down into your belly and release any stored-up tension by breathing it away.

Either physically or through your imagination, sit or stand in the middle of the mandala. Imagine that you are the centre of a wheel, the hub, where each of the spokes extends outwards forming the segments. All parts of the wheel are connected, and work together enabling the wheel to turn and move.

From your central position turn to face each of the directions one at a time, either in your mind's eye or physically placing your body to face the direction you're connecting with and then contemplate the question for each direction. This exercise can be completed in one sitting or if you prefer you can take a direction a day, week or month.

Each direction has a different energy to it and will offer different insights. Their messages can be received in many ways. You may see images, hear words, and have a sensation in your body. Whichever way you connect with the essence of each energy is perfect- there is no right or wrong way to do this.

You may like to have a notebook or journal handy to make notes on what you gleaned from each of the directions as you make your way around the mandala. A free printable PDF of the mandala is available at www.guidedbylove.co.uk

Your journey begins at 1 Water facing North.

1 Water- North

Connect to potential.

Imagine a crisp, cold evening in midwinter. Snow is on the ground knee-deep, and you are cosy inside wrapped up in a blanket. All activities have slowed down giving you the opportunity to be still, quiet and check in with yourself.

From this quiet, still and relaxed place ask yourself the following questions:

- ★ What's my direction in life?
- ★ Where is the flow of life leading me?
- ★ Am I connected to my potential and being led by it or am I treading water?
- ★ Look back at your achievements and successes. Assess your qualities, abilities and strengths (see your archetype) and how they can be best used.

Allow yourself to gain a deep sense of where your talents and dreams can lead you.

8 Earth- Northeast

Connect to integrity

Imagine a beautiful Mountain rising from the ground bathed in moonlight. Strong and majestic, supporting and nurturing all the life living on it.

Being a mountain of strength and knowledge

Cultivating a solid sense of self so that you can stand in your truth provides the stability and emotional intelligence you need to make balanced choices and decisions.

Ask yourself- *"Who am I, where do I stand and what do I stand for?"*

The ability to stand firm in self-certainty enables you to be present and nurturing to yourself and others without neediness or co-dependency.

Allow yourself the space and time to reflect and meditate on your values, boundaries and non-negotiables.

3 Tree- East

Connect to sources of inspiration

Imagine walking barefoot on the grass to feel the dew rise in March and watch the sunrise. Feel the energy rising around you. Note your feelings at the beginning of a new day. Ready to move forward, enthused and motivated.

★ What inspires you to grow; personally, professionally and spiritually?

★ Who inspires you- what seeds of possibility have been passed down through your ancestors and teachers?

★ Inspiration equals possibilities.

★ What ideas arise within you when you allow yourself to be inspired?

3 Tree is the energy of rapid growth, unimpeded by obstacles. Just like the shoots of plants that are so driven to be alive that they break through concrete.

Allow yourself to create a vision for your life.

4 Tree- Southeast

Connect to creativity and resourcefulness

In your mind's eye (or literally) go and stand or sit next to a tree in late spring. You can hear the birds singing, squirrels leaping and chatting whilst curiously exploring. Put your back against its strong trunk and feel your strength rising within you, supported by the tree.

Creativity comes in many forms from poetry and art to being resourceful. 4 Tree energy is an invitation to be open to what Life offers to you, especially when it is not what you expected.

When you become aware of and utilise the resources available to you, you grow and prosper. Once you have identified and acknowledged your resources, the next phase is planning how to use them mindfully and creatively.

Allow yourself to be aware of and open to the resources available to you. Note down what comes to mind.

9 Fire- South

Connect to your best most loving self

Relax in the midday sun in June and notice the flowers in full bloom. The vibrant colours, radiant heat and the brightness and activity make you feel vibrant. Become aware of your own energy moving to the surface, perhaps you get a sense of feeling more expressive, outgoing and social.

* ★ How do you show up in your best light? As your best self?
* ★ What enables you to shine brightly?
* ★ Ask yourself *"What's the most loving thing to do?"*

When we are in the 'spotlight' our motives become obvious to those around us.

Our guiding light in life gives us clarity and can burn away whatever is unnecessary in our lives.

Allow yourself to be guided by love.

2 Earth- Southwest

Connect to others and nurture relationships

It's lunchtime on a warm sunny day. You have plenty of time to savour the food and the company. You're in the mood to catch up and find out what's happening with the friends and family gathered. Is there anything to be done? Is any support or help needed?

We need love and connection to survive and thrive.

"The quality of our relationships determines the quality of our lives."

-Esther Perel.

★ What is the quality of your relationships?
★ How well do you relate to others?
★ Are you cultivating a deep sense of connection and intimacy or are you blocking it?

Allow yourself to be nourished and to nourish your relationships.

7 Metal- West

Connect to joy

It's sunset on an autumnal September day. As the sun goes down and dips below the horizon at the end of the day you consider and give thanks for all your achievements. This gives you a feeling of joy and prompts you to share the joy and celebrate.

Enjoy the fruition of your efforts.

★ What tasks and projects have you completed that have brought joy in their accomplishment?

The Lake (which symbolises 7 Metal) is like a pooling of resources that can be enjoyed as they are or used for developing further.

★ Realistically evaluate the results- what's their value?

Allow yourself to bathe in the joy of your accomplishments.

6 Metal- Northwest

Connect to support

It's dusk on a late autumn day, and as the darkness comes in you settle down for the evening. The contrast between day and night gives you pause for thought. You begin to consider your responsibilities and how best to utilise your resources and support structures.

Trusting that there is always help and support available when you need it.

6 Metal energy is associated with the father. He busies himself providing all the resources you need and ensuring that you are protected. He gives you encouragement, direction and discipline.

- ★ How are you staying within and managing your resources?
- ★ Is your giving and receiving balanced?

Allow yourself to be supported and held by others.

5 Earth (Centre)

Connect to your centre

Imagine sitting comfortably on the ground in the middle of a park, feeling supported by the Earth. You have a sense of stability and security and from that place you can make plans.

You are the centre of your world and therefore the most important person in it!

The centre connects to all the other directions or energies. This connection both resources the energies in your life and is resourced by them.

It's important to clear the clutter in your life and heal. To avoid extremes and learn to balance. And to take good care of yourself.

- ★ Where are you being thrown off-centre or giving your power away in your life?
- ★ In what ways can you come back to your centre?

Allow yourself to be the central element in your life.

21

A HORSE CALLED WENDY

BEING IN NATURE IS RESTORATIVE. IT HELPS YOU TO BE PRESENT BY offering you a feast for your five senses; sight, hearing, taste, smell and touch. Nature offers interesting sounds, smells and textures to explore. Whilst walking along if you intend to notice what you are experiencing you will find that there is so much going on.

One of my favourite places to go is the woods, ideally with a stream or river. Whilst I am walking, I will bring my attention to a range of things, one at a time. I may notice what kind of surface I'm walking on and how it feels. The hard gravel path that winds its way into the woods and transforms into a firm and sometimes claggy earthen base. The sound of scraping from the small stones of gravel underfoot compared to the wonderful sound your shoe makes when it's made a vacuum with the mud and your foot releases with a pop and a squelch.

Listening to the birds singing, the wind rustling the leaves on the trees, twigs snapping, water flowing, people chatting and dogs barking.

On a walk one day with Iris, rather than going our usual route and sitting on our favourite meditation bench, I suggested walking next to the river. I felt like water was calling me to listen, to go with the flow and let go of anything that needed to be released.

We stood on a wooden bridge, the sun warming our faces. I closed my eyes and listened to the water swirling, trickling and running under our feet at a fairly fast pace. The powerful and yet at the same time peaceful din was occurring beneath us, in front and behind us.

I opened my eyes and a flash of white caught my eye. In the distance walking up the hill in a kind of zig zag, somewhat unpredictable formation was a horse and its rider. The horse who from that angle looked quite large and muscular, like a Shire Horse was picking the route gingerly as though not to slip. Something told me that this horse and rider were not completely relaxed.

We watched as the horse meandered the twisting path towards us and upon seeing the water, reared up onto her back legs whilst her rider calmly held on. The horse, who we could now see was quite young stood well away from the water's edge and seemed to have no interest at all in crossing.

"Come on Wendy, you can do it," said the rider.

Wendy didn't budge an inch.

The rider looked over to us and explained that the horse had frightened her young, 8-year-old owner by rearing up and so she had been tasked with de-sensitising and socialising Wendy. Wendy was beautiful, black and white with a long fluffy mane and tail and sporting feathers on her legs, a Mini Gypsy Vanner.

This splendid symbol of power and strength, the kind of strength that can carry you forward, wearing the colours of balance, was anxious.

Wendy's rider was the epitome of calm and compassion, she knew that Wendy could cross this unknown body of muddy water and gently coaxed her. It was a dance of one hoof forward and two hooves back. Whenever Wendy would attempt to reverse or retreat, her guide softly told her it was OK and that they were not going back. Wendy tentatively moved forward a small amount at a time, eating an occasional blade of grass.

"Have a sniff of the water Wendy. You know what it is and you'll like it when you get in" said her rider, encouraging her to put one foot in.

As Wendy splashed the feathers on the bottom of her front hooves at the very edge of the stream, Iris and I dismounted the bridge and went to the other side to support and cheerlead.

"Come on Wendy, you can do it" we all said enthusiastically. Her rider making lovely warm cooing type sounds as a form of encouragement.

After a few minutes of false starts Wendy raised her head and slowly made her way across.

Yay!!!! Well done, Wendy, Iris and I cheered and clapped as this beautiful little horse overcame her fear and slowly trod up the woodland path.

The take aways I got from this encounter were many, including:

♥ I trusted my intuition, the inner nudge that said "This way" as we took a different route.

Nudges come to me in the form of a loving and secure voice that feels safe. Even if I have a moment of doubt, when I receive a thought that pops into my head that is timely and gently directive, I have learnt to trust it. To follow its guidance. It often takes me down a path that I haven't explored before, metaphorically or physically.

These redirects or nudges always lead to something worth learning or exploring which is why I trust them. If I hadn't listened to the nudge, we wouldn't have had such a lovely experience with Wendy and her rider and indeed I wouldn't have then been able to share the story and my learnings with you.

You always have the answers within you, they are whispered and mirrored back to you through thoughts, feelings, intuition and deep knowings. Even when in your heart of hearts, you know the truth of a situation, it can be hard or even painful to accept and allow. To listen rather than resist. Although it can be scary, if you allow it, life can show you new paths that will greatly exceed your expectations and take you to higher heights of happiness and contentment.

♥ Wendy couldn't see the bottom of the water and yet trusted that she would be OK

In life you don't always know what is at the top of the staircase or round the corner and in order to know, you need to take steps. One at a time. The more steps you take, the more information you have. The more you learn to trust that life is for you and loves you, the deeper your trust will be.

Wendy's ability to walk into unknown waters was aided by a few factors. She had experienced water before; she had built up some trust with her rider and she had an innate sense of her natural qualities.

Gypsy Vanner's were originally bred to pull caravans and are impressive cart horses. Due to their strength and calm, mild mannered characters, they can turn their hands to a range of purposes from competing in dressage shows to pulling carriages for pleasure.

Wendy, just like an acorn is designed to grow into a mighty Oak, naturally followed her inner design and used her strength and calm to take her rider across the river. Despite her initial reluctance, she drew upon her skills and with the encouragement of her guide, who reminded Wendy of her own natural calmness, conquered the river.

You won't always be able to see what you are walking into in life. Trust yourself and surround yourself with people who are grounded and supportive. Move through the fear to enable you to travel through the murk into crystal clear waters. Give yourself the opportunity to experience the wonders that await you on the other side of the unknown. Step in.

* ♥ Although she wanted to go back, she persisted and went forward, through the unknown waters.

I can imagine there have been times in your life, as there have been in mine, where you wish you could go back to how it was before. Where it seemed safer, more secure and perhaps happier? Whilst it is lovely to reminisce, the past is behind you and the future is calling you forward.

You have a choice in the present moment to take what you have learnt from the past and either put things down or take them with you. Even a cart horse can only carry so much before the weight becomes too much.

I encourage you to put down the heavy weights of regret, remorse and resentment. To lighten your load and step forwards. To avoid the temptation to go back to what was and explore what is out there for you now.

Moving forwards takes courage, strength and persistence. Determination grows like a passionate spark that ignites within you and fuels the fire. The spark is unique to you. It may be the excitement that grows when you think about a more empowered, assertive version of you and how your life can be enriched by this new way of being.

It could be the feeling that opens your heart wide open when you imagine a new healthy relationship that offers true love, deep connection and is secure.

Whatever your spark of intention is, use it at times when you feel yourself wanting to shrink and go back. Those moments when your boundaries are being tested, your resolve is wavering and remember that "the best way out is through" or as Thich Nhat Hahn says, *"the best way out, is in"*, meaning go inwards to discover the answers to your quandaries.

* ♥ She was a symbol of strength and balance

Wendy epitomised strength with her strong, muscular build and the ability to transport a person on her back. Her rider's weight evenly balanced to help carry the load. Even though Wendy was outwardly strong, she still needed to draw upon her inner strength to overcome her anxiety about crossing the river.

You are stronger than you think you are, I promise. As the Japanese proverb states- fall down 7 times and stand up 8. Choose to never give up hope and always follow your dreams. Focus on what you can do rather than what you have no control over.

Until you are in a situation, you never really know how strong you can be, for yourself and for your family. I certainly surprised myself about how much strength I could muster to do the hard things I had to do. Days when I didn't want to face the world or leave the house and still found the courage to go to the shops, make the difficult phone calls and hold my children in their despair. All without crumbling or hardening.

I balanced my strength and courage with nurturing and compassion. I allowed myself days to cry and grieve, to miss and wonder. To hold myself with compassion as I berated myself for shoulda, coulda, woulda's that eventually morphed into acceptance, gratitude and peace.

Other days I was a tower of strength, with little hints on the outside of the pain I was in and the experience I was enduring as I put my best foot forward and stepped into unknown territory.

One of the biggest things I had to do was swallow my pride and ask for government assistance. I had to be strong and at the same time balance that with being vulnerable. Having worked as professional Careers Adviser for over a decade until 2014, being on the 'other side of the desk' felt completely demoralising. I had the grace to know though, that the lovely lady across from me, was there to help and I was extremely grateful for the support afforded to me.

- ♥ Her rider showed her love, patience, compassion and softly supported her.

When your system is in overdrive from anxiety, fear and anguish, soothing is the best way to heb you move forwards. Self-soothing or soothing offered by someone dse enables you to relax, let go and put things into perspective.

Love can be shown in so many ways from a gentle squeeze of the hand, being accompanied to something daunting and someone making dinner for you. Love is like a warm comfort blanket that holds you close and enables you to soften.

Patience involves taking the time and not rushing. Tolerating something that may take a while to complete. Wendy's rider took all the time she needed to cross the stream. She didn't get frustrated or annoyed, rather gently encouraged and persisted

In times of change a huge dollop of patience is likely to be required. There were many times when I had to dig deep into my reserves of patience as I healed and grew as a person. The times when I wanted to go ahead with moving on with my life and was thwarted by circumstances, grief and other people's actions.

Compassion is being sensitive to the emotional suffering of yourself and others. It is recognising that a certain amount of gentleness and help will make a difference to the suffering involved. To help in a constructive way.

Wendy's rider showed compassion to her steed by exposing her safely and slowly to new experiences that she anticipated Wendy would come across in the future. She was aware of her background and purpose and wanted her to succeed. She knew the best way to do that was to support her through the challenges likely to be faced so that in similar situations Wendy would feel more confident and access her inner reserves where necessary.

♥   Her rider reassured her and offered words of affirmation.

Words are powerful, coupled with the intonation and intention behind them they are magic. Affirmations are statements designed to uplift, empower and brighten your outlook. They are positive, inspiring and often action orientated.

Examples are:

- ♥ I embrace the rhythm of life and let it unfold.
- ♥ I focus on action to create the life I want.
- ♥ I know my intuition will always take me in the right direction.
- ♥ I can become anything I put my mind to.

Wendy may not have known what the words meant and yet Wendy visibly relaxed more and more when her rider stroked her, talked to her and gave her little loving nudges. She continued to reassure Wendy until she felt confident to put her feet into the water. Her tone was upbeat and encouraging, there wasn't a hint of anger or despondence.

I know I respond better when I speak to myself or am spoken to with respect, honesty and kindness. When I am encouraged and built up, I feel motivated to act, take a risk or help in some way.

Imagine if Wendy's rider took the opposite approach and berated her, shouted at her and put her down. The little horse would remain in her threat system and perhaps be even more anxious and skittish than she was before, thus serving no one.

On the days when your inner critic rears its head and you get frustrated or mad at yourself, remember please that in every moment you can begin again. Reach for gentle ways to talk to yourself in difficult moments. You can even go back to something you have said and restate it using new words from a more enlightened perspective.

- ♥ Nature and life offer lessons wherever we are willing to take a moment to notice.

Life is always talking to you.

I believe that if you open your heart and mind up to the possibility that there are lessons and signs being offered to you daily that your life can be richer. Taking notice of what is happening around you and what you are feeling can give you clues as to whether you are in alignment to your true self or not. Being in alignment offers more opportunities to live your best life, utilising your strengths and not being held back by challenging circumstances, thoughts or beliefs. To have an underlying sense that all is well and that you have the tools and support to overcome any trials.

Watching and interacting with Wendy and her rider gave me an abundance of beautiful lessons. That experience lasted around 25 minutes on one day. Life is full of these, if you choose it to be so.

I watched a programme about a scheme in Africa where researchers and conservationists were designing inexpensive and easy to use devices to help keep elephants and humans who were living in the same area together safe.

The researchers used the power of nature to help them come up with some ingenious ideas, as well as using their knowledge of what elephants do and don't like. They discovered that elephants are repelled by the sound of bees as they hate being stung so they installed real and electronic beehives around the villagers crops to keep all involved safe. The plus side also being that the villagers now had honey to eat and sell.

They also observed that the elephants dug up a particular root to quench their thirst when water was in short supply and so the villagers used the roots to feed and save their animals during droughts. These observations enabled the humans to grow their crops and live safely without them being trampled on. Now that the elephants were no longer a huge threat, the villagers could relax and observe their natural ways to sustain themselves. A wonderful example of nature offering lessons for peaceful living.

This programme reminded me of and validated my approach to life since my separation. That you don't have to use negative, unloving or cruel tactics to get what you want. You can use your natural resources, guided by love to keep everyone safe and away from harm. It was a reminder that boundaries are necessary to uphold peace and that kindness, respect and love create a harmonious environment.

The Three Gifts

From the experience with a little horse called Wendy, I formulated the three gifts; presence, experience and sharing:

1st Gift -Presence

Being present, mindful and noticing what is around you, really taking the time to slow down and be aware is a real gift. When you are in the present moment, you are in your power. You can focus on what you have control over right now, including your thoughts and actions. The past is behind you and the future is yet to come and so concentrating on the present can help you feel confident, content and calm.

2nd Gift -Experience

Once you are in the present moment then your experience can be fully appreciated. Full technicolour instead of black, white and grey. Experiences can be missed, can fly past you if you skip the first gift of presence. Not all experiences will be pleasant, some may be painful however they are still a gift- an opportunity for growth. Perhaps to stretch your comfort zone, to release you from being stuck, to give you insights about yourself or a situation.

3rd Gift -Sharing

Sharing connects you to others. It gives you insights and joy to recall and relay your experience. Hearing yourself talk or seeing your words on a page can highlight thoughts and feelings that have been playing in the background ready to be brought forward and illuminated. Equally your story is likely to invoke the recipient's imagination too. You never really know the impact a story can have on someone else. It may remind them of a happy memory or offer the last piece to a puzzle through understanding a familiar concept through a new lens. A wonderful gift indeed.

22

DRAINS AND RADIATORS

YOUR ENERGY CAN BE DEPLETED BY CERTAIN ACTIVITIES AND FILLED up by others. Energy drains are activities or thoughts that you have in daily life that drain your energy and lower your mood. Imagine your energy draining out of you, being sucked down a plug hole. That feeling of heaviness, apathy and exhaustion. You cannot live your purpose with too many energy drains.

Radiating activities are the ones where you feel joy, contentment and worth. The ones that fill you up and enable you to radiate or send out your positive energy and know that it is appreciated and acknowledged.

For example, if someone calls you and asks you to do something, I invite you to pay attention to what your mind and body does. If it is a likely energy drain you will feel a sinking, heavy feeling accompanied by unenthusiastic thoughts.

If someone else calls you and asks you to do something and your chest raises with a light feeling accompanied by enthusiastic thoughts this is a great sign it will be a positive experience that radiates energy.

Not everything you are required to do in life is pleasurable, that said, your energy can give you clues as to who, what and when to use your precious energy.

If you are feeling particularly drained by an activity, where possible either limit the time you commit to it or wait until your energy is more balanced. It's always better to make choices and decisions from a neutral, centred and balanced place than from an overly negative or positive place. To utilise your energy efficiently to gain the best results.

One of the best decisions I made to lower my stress levels, to honour my energy and to take a burden off my shoulders was to have convenient, yummy and healthy food delivered weekly. Utilising a kit-based food delivery service has saved me hours of anguish over what meals to make and trips to the supermarket. We can sit and choose what we fancy to eat during the week and then sit back and relax. This is the Pareto Principle in action.

The Pareto Principle

The Pareto Principle or the 80/20 rule suggests that using 20% of focussed time on an activity produces 80% of the work. To identify and prioritise your best assets (in this case your energy) and use them efficiently to create maximum value.

You can use the 80/20 rule to prioritise the tasks that you need to get done during the day. The idea is that out of your entire task list, completing 20% of those tasks will result in 80% of the impact you can create for that day.

The tricky thing is that if you have been in an unbalanced relationship or work situation, you are probably used to giving away 80% of your energy and receiving 20%. This may be a revelation to you and so you will need to practice resetting this energy imbalance in your favour.

To do this, make a list of all the things that you need to get done today or this week. Then identify which of those tasks have the highest impact on your energy, quality of life and goals. Do any of your tasks result in a reduction of suffering, for example to feel reassured by talking to the bank about your finances? Doing some exercise to relieve tension? Making a meal plan so that you feel organised?

Find Your Truth

Loose boundaries often stem from a lack of self-worth or a sense that you must 'prove' yourself. By putting down striving, trying and self-improvement, you can discover your truth. Permit yourself to recognise the truth of who you are underneath all the layers of expectations and burdens.

Ask yourself, *"Who would I be and what would my life look like if I gave myself permission to live my truth?"* Focus on your skills, gifts, strengths, wishes and dreams. If you feel called to share those gifts, trust that the right people will be drawn to you because of who you are.

You cannot be improved because you are already a masterpiece. Expressing yourself and creating the life you want is the path to living with ease. A life of comfort, lightness and inner peace.

Give yourself permission and the gift to live a life of ease.

A life where you stand in your truth, your power and strength.

And in doing so you will draw to you true friends and true reciprocal relationships.

Your energy and your truth is more important than manners. More important than attempting to please others. It's so important for you to make sure that your mental, emotional and social well-being is at the centre or the focus of your life. By making yourself a priority, Life, the Universe will reflect that choice back to you. Therefore, you will draw towards you experiences, opportunities, connections and relationships where you are also a priority.

A Common Tale

It's a hard pill to swallow when you haven't seen something coming. When your best efforts made in the name of love are thwarted. It's gut-wrenching, anguish-provoking, and breaks your heart and soul into pieces.

You're left feeling shocked, stupid, and vulnerable.

Whilst you were pouring all your love, attention and gifts into your relationship, they were soaking it all up and planning their exit.

When something is easy to recognise, you don't get easily tricked. It's when the 'near enemies' of emotions are at play you can be duped. It can seem like these 'near enemies' are cultivating connection, when in fact they are sabotaging the relationship and driving disconnection from yourself and others. Then you tend to turn pain inwards and think something is wrong with you.

The near enemy of love is attachment.

The near enemy of equanimity is indifference.

The happy ending that can be written into this tale is you can learn and grow from this experience. You can pick yourself up, dust yourself off and be your own project. And once complete you can choose someone to love who is already whole, happy and content and allow them to fill you up as much as you do them.

CONCLUSION

Relaxed, content and feeling uplifted by the sunshine, I was filled with an impending sense of upcoming space, freedom and relief. Soon to be finalising the end of my marriage and moving to a new home. I was looking out of the kitchen window, whilst washing up. Admiring my garden, taking in the array of colours, and finding myself amused by the birds popping in to grab a bite to eat. Music playing in the background.

I imagined shoelaces being pulled together and tied in a bow. That all the threads of the last couple of years were coming together. Just like when the kids learnt to tie their shoelaces. I remember the concentration on Iris's face as she carefully prepared a loop with one lace and then attempted to coordinate her small fingers with the other lace to make a bow. She was delighted and felt so accomplished and contented when she could do it by herself and we now had more choice of shoes instead of only Velcro fastening.

A song in the background got my attention and caught me off guard. It touched my heart bringing a few gentle tears to my eye. The singer expresses tenderly a story of love and heartache. The gentle tears were from acceptance. Acceptance that life is different now and that I have no resistance to that. I noticed a bubbling excitement rising from my tummy signalling a curiosity about what will now take up the space that has been created. And relief that I could truly let go and be confident about my forward journey.

Where before that type of song would have brought me to my knees in floods of tears, in this new moment, it was a fleeting bittersweet reminder that:

Everything is good

Nothing can go wrong

All my needs are met

I am safe

I am loved.

And a reminder that:

- ♥ You can love someone and choose not to be with them.
- ♥ You can recognise the truth of a relationship and choose to keep responding with love.
- ♥ You can warmly remember the memories, whilst looking to the future you want to create.
- ♥ You can maintain boundaries and hold space for your self-worth and self-compassion.

A warm glow of pride radiated from my heart when I understood how far I had come. When I was able to discern the contrast of a time when I would have contracted and crumbled and now, I allow expansion. Instead of shrinking and allowing judgment, blame and self-criticism to pervade my mind and heart. I now invite curiosity, love and new perspectives that enable me to grow. Along with a healthy dose of self-compassion to keep the weeds from taking over the flowers.

I believe that everything happens for a reason even if at the time you feel bewildered and shocked by outcomes that you were not prepared for. I believe that there is a design for your life with lessons peppered through it, for you to embrace. As well as gifts to receive. This beautiful, messy life is a journey of self-discovery and growth. If you allow it, life guided by love places you on a path of deeper self-awareness, so that you can live authentically and in your truth.

Be proud of yourself. You have full permission to walk with your head held high. To feel all the feelings and have days when the tissues are required. To know that life is a journey, and every day is a school day. To have pride in yourself for not staying stuck and for embracing change.

I'll leave you for now by posing a couple of questions:

- ♥ If you knew that they were never going to change, what would you do?
- ♥ What can you take away from the change, instead of focusing on what the change is taking away from you?

I'm excited for my next chapters, and I am excited for yours.

All my love

Ava x

ACKNOWLEDGEMENTS

I am truly blessed to have amazing family and friends around me who support and encourage my endeavours. Without the warm hugs, love, chocolate, late-night S.O.S calls and various skill sets this book would not have materialised. What started as a series of journal entries and stories transformed into a record of my journey, which for you dear reader, I sincerely hope has helped or inspired you in some small way.

I thank you, the awesome person that holds this book in their hands, for picking it up and trusting that I had something of value to share with you. I'm sending you love and wish you all the peace and happiness in the world.

Huge thanks to Stacey McDonald my story coach who patiently and wisely teased out more emotion and depth from within me that I knew was possible. Thank you for expertly alchemising my thoughts into words, enabling me to share my truth and heal.

Much gratitude to my editor Dianna Emerson whose eagle eyes and careful stewarding of the integrity of my writing, polished my words like a diamond.

To Mandy Nicolson, mentor and friend who inspires me greatly and whose book *The Life I Won* was a catalyst to writing my own, thank you for everything.

Many thanks to Jean Haner for introducing me to the wonderful art of Nine Star Ki and to Rex Lasselle and Michael Becherer for deepening my knowledge and admiration for its transformative effects and applications.

Shout out to the fabulous folk in my Facebook group dedicated to this book, Guided By Love, who have been on this writing journey with me from the beginning, cheerleading, supporting and encouraging me. Thank you for keeping me accountable to get to the finish line, I hope you enjoy the result.

Thank you to all at Balboa Press for enabling me to turn my musings into a real book that I can admire with pride on my bookshelf.

The beautiful Nine Star Ki illustrations were created by my talented friend Lizzie Cairns of Blinkin' Imp. Thank you, Petal. The lovely illustrations of Maya and Wendy were accurately and beautifully drawn by Gail Armstrong, Start With a Doodle, many thanks to you.

The gorgeous cover was created by Vicki H Nicolson who has an incredible and intuitive skill of taking an idea and creating magical imagery.

My family is my biggest joy and so naturally I would like to honour them here. I am lucky to come from a line of strong women on both sides, many of whom enjoyed the art of storytelling. My great grandmother and my grandmother on my mother's side were beautiful poets, thank you for passing along the joy of writing. My grandmother on my dad's side was a prolific reader, particularly of Westerns.

To my mum for her unflinching love and support (and the occasional editing), you are my rock.

To my dad for modelling true love and maintaining kindness in adversity.

To my children, my heart bursts with love and pride in having the privilege to be your mum. Thank you for your patience whilst I wrote this book and rose from the ashes of our loss. I'm in awe at the incredible, warm, wise and courageous people you are. I love you to the moon and back.

ABOUT THE AUTHOR

AVA WOODS (a pen name, to protect those in the book) offers gentle, yet profound guidance on love and connection, teaching you to stand in your truth and follow your inner love song. She lives in beautiful Northumberland, UK with her family and fur babies.

With her writing, coaching and healing gifts she leads women through a transformative experience aligning them to their natural power and strengths. Weaving a path to empowerment, clarity and self-compassion through her encouraging conversational sessions.

She consults the ancient wisdom of Nine Star Ki, a foundational tool in her work. She has studied this insightful cosmology for over a decade and has been mentored by world-renowned teachers in this art.

Utilising her toolbox of alchemy, the author is skilled at creating a safe space for self-discovery and is a container for change. A great listener, with a kind open heart and an intuition for potential. She gently inspires you to connect with your own inner peace, self-love and balance, especially during times of unexpected change, loss and grief.

Sign up for the free Guided By Love newsletter to receive updates, quizzes and information at **www.guidedbylove.co.uk**

www. lindseyelms. com

Printed and bound by CPI Group (UK) Ltd, Croydon, CR0 4YY